INSIDE THE ANCIENT WORLD

SLAVERY IN ANCIENT ROME

MICHAEL MASSEY
AND PAUL MORELAND

M

MACMILLAN EDUCATION

First published 1978
Reprinted 1979, 1980

Published by
MACMILLAN EDUCATION LTD
Houndmills Basingstoke Hampshire RG21 2XS
and London
Associated companies in Delhi Dublin
Hong Kong Johannesburg Lagos Melbourne
New York Singapore and Tokyo

Filmset by Keyspools Ltd, Golborne, Lancashire

Printed in Hong Kong

British Library Cataloguing in Publication Data
Massey, Michael
Slavery in Ancient Rome.—(Inside the ancient world).
1. Slavery in Rome
I. Title   II. Series   111. Moreland, Paul
301.44'93'0937   HT863
ISBN 0-333-18317-7

Contents

Illustrations

The authors and publisher wish to acknowledge the following photograph sources:

Alinari-Giraudon p.72; British Museum p.6; Cambridge University Press p.74; Cinema International Corporation p.60; Giraudon p.41; Landesmuseum Trier p.51; Mansell Collection pp.20, 35, 39, 53, 71; P. Moreland p.43; Musée Royal de Mariemont p.68; Museum of Classical Archaeology, Cambridge p.10; University of Cambridge (Archaeology & Anthropology) p.30; Roger Wood p.37.

The publishers have made every effort to trace the copyright holders, but if they have inadvertently overlooked any, they will be pleased to make the necessary arrangements at the earliest opportunity.

I

Introduction

In a play by Plautus, the Roman dramatist, a slave called Gripus speaks to the audience about what he would do if he were free:

This is what I'm going to do. I've got it all worked out. When I'm free, I'll buy some land, a house, slaves and the rest, and start up in business as a merchant shipper. I'll be famous, a king of kings. I'll buy a boat to amuse myself, like all the millionaires, and cruise around from port to port. When everyone knows me well, I'll build a great new city and call it after me – Gripopolis! It will remind people of all the great things I've done; it will be the capital of a great Empire. No doubt about it – I'm thinking really big.

[Plautus, *Rudens* 925 ff]

Of course his dreams do not come true. Nevertheless this speech is one of the rare moments when a slave speaks to us directly about his thoughts and ambitions. Gripus is only a character in a play, but many of the slaves in the audience must have felt and thought as he did about freedom. So, what was it like to be a slave? What did it mean to lose your freedom and be someone else's possession?

The idea that people can be bought and sold like pieces of property is one that we are not used to. That people can be treated as objects with no legal rights is something that we may find hard to understand; it is certainly something that we would not tolerate in our own society. To the ancient Romans it seemed more natural. They found it easier to accept that their own race was superior to others. They even thought that other races were born to be slaves. It is not difficult to discover what the Romans thought about slavery because they made many references to it in their writings. They tell us how people became slaves, how they were treated, what their duties were, how they obtained their freedom, what happened to them afterwards. They do not tell us why no-one thought about abolishing slavery, nor why it was less widespread towards the end of the Roman

1 A comic slave actor

Empire. Most significant of all, they do not tell us what it was really like to be a slave.

Most of these ideas would never have occurred to Gripus. Perhaps he had never even thought very seriously about whether slavery was wrong. His own words show that he accepted slavery as a natural part of life – when he is rich he will have slaves in his turn. In the meantime he is quite content to serve his master and accept the rewards and punishments which are handed out to him. Slaves like Gripus served their masters in many different ways. In town they performed the daily chores of cleaning, waiting and cooking as well as having more responsible tasks as messengers, attendants, librarians, copyists, secretaries, tutors and doctors. In the country they were farm-labourers, but the more skilled slaves also tended the olives and vines. If they gained their freedom they often bought small businesses with money they had saved. Many joined clubs especially for slaves and freedmen, and enjoyed a full social life (see chapter 4). The life of a slave appears to have been tolerable under a kind master, as Cicero was. Cicero accepted the idea of slavery and saw to it that a friend's slave, who had run away, was traced in Asia. Nevertheless he showed a humane attitude towards most of his slaves, especially his personal secretary, Tiro, whom he later freed (see chapter 5).

Not all slaves were as lucky as Tiro and some suffered harsh treatment at the hands of their masters (see chapter 4). Such poor conditions and treatment did cause some slave revolts (see chapter 6).

Peasant farmers and slave labour

From the above it can be seen that Roman society relied heavily on slaves. This reliance increased during the wars against Carthage – the Punic Wars – which were fought between 264 and 146 BC. During that time many peasant farmers-turned-soldiers returned home after years of fighting to find their farms destroyed and their lands neglected. The upper classes, on the other hand, grew rich from the spoils of war and invested their profits in the purchase of land, which was always considered the best way of using money to make more money. They bought up small farms, or secured them by less honest means, and developed them into large estates. These estates were worked by slaves. After each campaign prisoners of war who had been sold into slavery were cheap and in plentiful supply: they were regarded by rich landowners as an additional source of investment.

Peasant farmers could not compete with these landowners and their big estates. Forced to live in near-poverty, they found it difficult to raise families and it was not uncommon for them to have to sell their children into slavery or abandon them in infancy. Children who suffered the latter fate would, if found, probably be brought up as slaves. This explains why the size of the freeborn population remained about the same while, thanks to capture and purchase, the number of slaves increased. By the time of the Emperor Domitian (AD 81–96) some ninety per cent of the population of Rome is said to have been able to trace some freedmen in their ancestry. This is how the historian Appian describes the situation in writing about Italy of 133 BC:

The poor complained that they were prevented from making a living and were being reduced to extreme poverty as well as to childlessness (since they could not afford to bring up their children). Recalling the military service they had done to obtain their land, they felt angry that they should be deprived of their share of something they had all fought for. They spoke bitterly against the rich for preferring to use slaves instead of free men, men who were citizens and soldiers. [Appian, *The Civil Wars* I.1.10]

2

Sources of slaves

Slaves were brought to Rome from all parts of the Mediterranean World. There was no area or country that did not produce slaves for sale in Rome's markets. The majority of slaves were prisoners captured during the succession of wars by which Rome gradually added the Mediterranean countries to her Empire. Others became slaves as the result of capture by pirates or brigands, of being born into slavery, of being sold or exposed, or of being sentenced to slavery for crime.

It soon became clear to the Romans that slaves of different nationalities had different skills and talents to offer, and slave dealers therefore falsified the origins of their wares in order to obtain a better price for them. Greek slaves were highly prized for their supposed intelligence and skill. Many slave-dealers therefore gave their slaves Greek names no matter where they had come from. We find, for example, a German slave with the Greek name Hermes, a Phrygian slave-girl with the name Athenais, a Jewish woman called Paramone, a slave-boy from Gaul with the Greek name Argoutis, and even a negro slave-girl with the two Greek names Atalous and Eutychia. We also find slaves with Greek names coming from Spain, Dalmatia, Sardinia, Africa and Thrace. This situation has made it difficult to work out where slaves came from.

The evidence we have does prove some important points. Firstly, only one in eight of all slaves came from countries outside the Empire. Secondly, most slaves who were found in any one part of the Empire had probably been born there. This does not, however, prove their race since their parents may well have been born elsewhere.

As we have said, the Romans came to expect different talents and skills from slaves of different nationalities. In this extract Catullus has just returned from a year's service in the Roman province of Bithynia on the Black Sea. When he meets his friends, they ask him how it went. He tells them, not too well:

'But,' they said, 'you did at least bring back some litter-bearers? Isn't that where they come from?' [Catullus, X]

It is now time to consider a little more closely how and why a person became a slave. There were, as we saw at the beginning of this chapter, various possibilities, but capture in war was the most likely reason.

Capture in war

This is what the historian Livy has to say about the fate of some prisoners of war after the capture of their camp:

On the next day the centurions and cavalrymen drew lots for the prisoners. They received one each, except for those whose bravery had been outstanding who were given two. The rest of the prisoners were sold by auction. [Livy, IV 34]

In another passage Livy writes:

Of the 10,000 free men captured, the Roman commander Scipio released those who were citizens of New Carthage, but decided that 2,000 craftsmen who had been taken prisoner were to become slaves of the Roman people . . . He handed over to the fleet the rest of the able-bodied inhabitants and slaves to serve as extra oarsmen. [Livy, XXVI 47]

In this case Scipio was clearly losing no time in putting some of the prisoners to good use. Sometimes more drastic action was taken against a defeated enemy. Julius Caesar, while fighting in Gaul, wanted to teach one of the local tribes a lesson for imprisoning his ambassadors:

He decided to take stronger measures against the Veneti to make the other Gallic tribes more careful in future about respecting the rights of ambassadors. He therefore executed all their leading citizens and sold the rest into slavery. [Caesar, *Gallic War* III 16]

Caesar was nothing if not ruthless when he wanted to be.

The total number of prisoners-of-war captured during the Republic was obviously considerable. Each campaign would have brought a fresh supply of slaves. The figures we have for captives are no doubt rounded up to the nearest impressive digit in each case, but they do give an indication of the number of slaves that could be involved. Here is a selection from the list of figures available:

197 BC	Macedonia	5,000
177 BC	Illyria	5,000 or more
177 BC	Sardinia	80,000 (killed or captured)
167 BC	Epirus	150,000
146 BC	Carthage	50–60,000
102–1 BC	against the Teutones & Cimbri	140,000

Caesar is said to have taken nearly a million prisoners during his nine years of campaigning in Gaul (58–49 BC) – though this figure has been disputed (and has been put as low as 150,000).

2 *Captives depicted on a triumphal arch at Carpentras in southern France*

Cicero writing to Atticus, his literary friend and banker, in 54 BC – at the time of Caesar's second 'invasion' of Britain – does not expect British slaves to be of exceptional quality, but his letter does reveal what people at Rome wanted from foreign conquest:

The outcome of the British campaign is eagerly awaited . . . but we now know that there is not a trace of silver in the island and that the only hope of plunder is slaves – and I don't think you're expecting to find any literary or musical geniuses amongst them! [Cicero, *Letters to Atticus* IV 16]

Under the Emperor Augustus there was a period of comparative peace and a drastic reduction in the number of new slaves coming on to the market. But the supply did not dry up altogether. At the end of the Jewish War of A D 66–70, during the reign of Vespasian, we are told by the military historian Josephus that the total number of prisoners taken in that war was 97,000 (*The Jewish War* VI 9).

Piracy and brigandage

Second to war as a source of slaves was piracy. In the past Carthage had policed the western half of the Mediterranean to keep the area safe for her trading enterprises, and in the eastern half the trading stations of Rhodes and Egypt had performed the same service. After the destruction of Carthage in 146 BC, and the decline of Rhodes and Egypt, there was nothing to deter the pirates from their profitable business. Rome's fleet was never considered a major part of her fighting services and before Pompey's campaign in 66 BC Roman efforts to deal with the pirates had not met with much success.

In addition to plundering cargoes, the pirates captured passengers and crews and even kidnapped people from towns and villages along the coast. The most notorious group were the Cilician pirates who operated from the coast of Asia Minor. Prisoners were sold by the pirates as slaves unless a worthwhile ransom could be collected. This source of slaves was not questioned at Rome.

One group of pirates, however, made a serious mistake in ransoming one prisoner. In 76 BC they captured the young Julius Caesar who was on his way to Rhodes to study oratory. Immediately after his ransom had been paid he manned some ships, captured the pirates and had them crucified – a punishment he had threatened them with when he was their prisoner.

The pirates caused considerable disruption to Rome's trade and the extent of their daring may be seen from a speech of Cicero's in 66 BC:

Do I need to tell you that people coming from foreign nations were taken prisoner, that even Roman ambassadors had to be ransomed from the pirates? Do I need to remind you that famous cities like Cnidus or Colophon or Samos and countless others were captured by them, when you are aware that your own harbours ... are under their control? Haven't you heard that the harbour of Caieta ... was plundered by the pirates under the praetor's very eyes? And that the pirates carried off the children of that self-same man who had previously fought against them? Why mention the disaster at Ostia – when almost under your very nose a fleet that was important enough to have a consul in command was captured and sunk by the pirates?

[Cicero, *On the Manilian Law* 32–3]

Piracy was often a cover name for the slave trade. Large numbers of barbarians were sold over the borders of the Empire to Roman slave traders, most of them having been taken prisoner in tribal warfare in their own country.

BRIGANDAGE

Within Italy itself brigands, usually runaway slaves or ex-soldiers, made travel without an escort a hazardous affair. A man could be captured, sold to a slave-dealer and spend the rest of his life in the slave barracks of a farm. If his relatives found him, it would only be by chance. From time to time the areas frequented by brigands were swept by soldiers, and laws were passed forbidding people to carry arms except in self-defence:

Augustus remedied many of the threats to law and order which had arisen as a result of the lawless period of the civil wars or had sprung up in time of peace. For gangs of robbers openly went around armed with swords – worn in self-defence, of course. They seized travellers, both free and slave, and sold them off to the slave barracks of landowners ... Augustus, therefore, stationed troops in the most dangerous areas to curb their activities and also organised inspections of the slave barracks. [Suetonius, *Augustus* 32]

The problem was never fully dealt with, as we can see from a letter of the Younger Pliny:

You write that Robustus, a distinguished Roman knight, travelled as far as Ocriculum (about 15 kilometres north of Rome) with my friend Attilius Scaurus and then vanished without trace ... I suspect that something has happened to him as befell my fellow townsman, Metilius Crispus. I had arranged his promotion to centurion and when he was leaving I had given him 40,000 sesterces to buy his equipment and uniform. However, after he had gone I didn't receive a single letter from him nor did I hear of his death. Whether he was murdered by his slaves or together with them isn't certain. What is certain is that neither Crispus nor any of his slaves has been seen since. [Pliny the Younger, *Letters* VI 25]

In this case the money may have caused his disappearance but he was never heard of again.

The danger in the more remote parts of the Empire was much greater. Kidnapping had been very common in the East, especially in Asia and Syria – so much so that the name Syrian almost meant a slave. The island of Delos was the trading centre for the East and was very convenient both for the pirates of Cilicia and for the slave trade from Asia and Syria. Strabo, a geographer writing about the beginning of the Empire, has this to say about the island:

It was the exportation of slaves that persuaded most of the pirates to undertake their evil but very profitable trade. Slaves were easily caught, and a large, rich slave-market was not far away – namely Delos. Delos could receive and send away 10,000 slaves on the same day. As a result a saying grew up: 'Merchant, sail in, unload your ship; everything has been sold'.

[Strabo 14.5.2.]

The daily figure is an impressive one and, even if we are tempted to doubt it, 10,000 is perhaps not impossible for a good day's trade.

Home-rearing

Although slaves could not marry legally, they could with their owner's permission live together as man and wife. Any children they had became the property of that owner. The same was true of children born of master and slave girl. Children of such unions were called 'home-born' slaves (*vernae*). A *verna* was generally better treated than other slaves and, if he were born in a rich man's house, stood a reasonable chance of being trained for scholarly or professional jobs (see p. 46). Even if he could not be employed in his master's household, a trained slave would fetch a higher price on the market.

In the Republic the breeding of slaves was not a regular practice; but it did occur. Talking about Cato the Elder (234–149 BC), the biographer Plutarch states:

Cato also lent money to those of his slaves who wanted it; with it they would buy boys, and after training and teaching them at their master's expense they would sell them again after a year. Cato would keep many of these trained boys for himself, crediting his slaves with the price offered by the highest bidder. [Plutarch, *Cato the Elder* 21]

Cicero and Atticus both had young slaves trained in their households, mainly for literary jobs such as readers and secretaries. Several of these lived on excellent terms with their master and, earning their freedom at an early age, continued to serve him with gratitude and friendship. Unfortunately we cannot prove that these slaves were homeborn, although several seem to have been. Cicero, writing to Atticus in January of 61 BC, says of one such trained slave:

As I write I feel rather distressed: my reader Sositheus, an agreeable chap, has died, and this has upset me perhaps more than the death of a slave ought to. [Cicero, *Letters to Atticus* I 12]

One might have thought that on the large farms of the Republic the breeding of home-born slaves would have been used as a method of replacing stock. But this was not so. Farm-owners, it seems, preferred to buy replacements, for the cost of maintaining and feeding infants born of slaves kept for breeding purposes was not considered worthwhile when slaves from war and piracy were to be had cheaply and in large numbers. However, when the supply from these sources was drastically cut, from the time of Augustus onwards, it did become profitable to breed and train slaves. Columella, who wrote a handbook on agriculture in about AD 60, tells us:

I have exempted from work the slave-women who deserve reward for producing a certain number of children. Occasionally, I have even granted them their freedom when they have brought up a lot of children.

[Columella, *On Agriculture* 1.8.19]

Further evidence is found in Petronius, writing in the middle of the first century AD. In his fictional novel *Satyricon*, Petronius humorously describes a dinner-party given by Trimalchio, a fabulously wealthy but boastful ex-slave. During the dinner-party Trimalchio's accountant reads out the following list:

26 July: Born on the estates at Cumae 30 males and 40 females. 500,000 pecks of wheat threshed and put away, 500 oxen broken in.

On the same day for insulting the guardian spirit of Gaius, our master, the slave Mithradates was crucified. [Petronius, *Satyricon* 53]

Petronius of course is grossly exaggerating, but the exaggeration would be pointless if it were not based on a fact of life at that time: that slaves were now being bred on the big estates.

Enslavement by other means

BY SALE

Could a Roman citizen sell himself or a child into slavery? Roman law expressly forbade the practice: it was an offence punishable by death to buy or sell a free person, knowing him to be such. Yet what is forbidden by law and what actually happens are often two different things. A poor person, in desperation, must have found it an attractive idea to sell himself or one or more of his children into slavery. At least a slave was fed!

We know that such things happened in the provinces. In 85–84 BC in Asia the Roman general Sulla by his heavy tax demands forced many parents to sell their children, and eventually themselves:

The tax-collectors and money-lenders plundered the people of Asia and reduced them to slavery. Parents were forced to sell their handsome sons and unmarried daughters. Towns had to sell the offerings in their temples, their paintings and their sacred statues. Finally, citizens had no recourse but to sell themselves into slavery as a means of paying their creditors.

[Plutarch, *Lucullus* 20]

No doubt some of these unfortunate provincials ended up in the slave-markets at Delos and elsewhere.

A similar thing happened in AD 29 to the Frisians, a tribe on the German frontier, who were partially under Roman control:

In the same year the Frisians across the Rhine broke the peace. The reason they did so was because of Roman greed rather than because they were rebelling against Roman control. Drusus had imposed a moderate tribute in view of their poverty: they were to supply ox-skins for military use. The local Roman commander interpreted this as buffalo hides . . . So first the Frisians handed over their cattle, then their lands, and finally their wives and children into slavery. [Tacitus, *Annals* IV 72]

We know that men also hired themselves out as gladiators, even though in doing so they faced death in the arena.

These examples show the desperate conditions sometimes suffered by the poor. Poverty must certainly have been one of the main reasons why a man would go to the length of selling himself or his children. However, one of the guests at that same dinner-party of Trimalchio's gave a different motive:

My father was a king in his own country. 'Why then are you a slave?' you ask. Because I went into slavery of my own accord. I preferred to be a Roman citizen rather than a tax-paying subject. [Petronius, *Satyricon* 57.4]

The desire for advancement to Roman citizenship was indeed great, but you had to be sure you could earn your freedom first!

It is a curious fact that the Romans should give the rights of a citizen to a freed slave. The reason can hardly have been generosity. Whatever the motive was, the practice seems unique in the ancient world and it caused comment and admiration from foreigners observing Roman customs. Freedmen and their rights are discussed in a later chapter but a comment from the poet Horace is worth noting here. He was the son of a freedman from a small town in southern Italy and his father wanted the best for his son:

And if my nature is only slightly blemished by a few minor faults, my father must take the credit. He was a poor man with only a small area of land but he refused to send me to the local school – where the sons of important centurions go. Instead he was courageous enough to take me to Rome to be taught the same as any knight or senator would have his son taught.

[Horace, *Satires* I 6.65–78]

BY EXPOSURE

Another way of becoming a slave was as the result of being exposed as an infant. Unwanted children could be abandoned and left to die. If found, they were most likely to be reared as slaves. Roman law permitted exposure – and, for that matter, abortion. The rich practised both, believing it to be common sense; in the case of the poor it was more a question of necessity, as Appian made clear in a passage already quoted in chapter 1. No doubt female children were more often exposed than male ones. Moreover, since the historian Tacitus bothers to say of the Jews that 'it is a crime among them to kill any new-born infant' (*Histories* V 5), it seems likely that the practice was common at Rome.

The Christian writers, as one might expect, condemned exposure. Tertullian (c. AD 160–240) comments:

And as for those people thirsting for Christian blood, how many of them have killed their own children ... Surely it is crueller to drown someone or to expose him to cold, starvation and the dogs? [Tertullian, *Apology* IX 6]

It was a Christian emperor who finally banned the practice.

Legally anyone who was enslaved as the result of exposure was still a free person. But the chances of his ever finding out, let alone proving that he was of free birth, must have been very slim – especially if he had been sent to a foreign land.

FOR SERIOUS CRIME

During the Empire a person might also be enslaved as a punishment for serious crime. Such an offender was usually condemned to serve in the mines or quarries – and could expect to die there. Pliny mentions a teacher who had been condemned to the mines for forgery. An alternative sentence was to be made to fight in the arena: here it was possible for a successful fighter to earn his release, but probably few managed this.

Crimes for which an individual could be enslaved included theft, robbery, sacrilege and arson. Occasionally an emperor had a person reduced to slavery:

Augustus had a Roman knight sold into slavery and all his possessions auctioned because he had cut off the thumbs of his two young sons to make them unfit for military service. [Suetonius, *Augustus* 24]

Augustus later freed this man and let him live in a remote part of the country. Titus (AD 79–81) was not so generous:

One of the evils of the time were the informers. Titus had these severely whipped and clubbed in the Forum and finally paraded across the arena. Some were put up for sale; others were sent to desert islands.

[Suetonius, *Titus* 8]

3

Marketing and numbers

Marketing slaves

Although the trade of a slave-dealer was considered to be a
disreputable one, it had its compensations in the rich profits that
could be made. The slaves were normally sold by auction and at Rome
the sales were held in the Forum near the temple of Castor.

So that bidders could see and inspect them, the slaves were
normally placed on raised platforms. Indeed purchasers usually took
care to have their chosen items stripped and inspected very carefully.
They even called in medical advisers or made the slave jump about to
show his fitness, such was their distrust of the dealers. Even so it was
hard to be sure about one's choice:

I have very great respect for your judgement . . . The slaves that I bought on
your advice look satisfactory. Whether they are honest remains to be seen,
and this in the case of slaves is best judged by what one hears about them
rather than by what one sees of them. [Pliny the Younger, *Letters* I 21]

Newly-imported slaves had their feet whitened with chalk, as we
learn from a reference in Pliny the Elder:

But the cheapest sort of chalk is the one we traditionally use to mark the
victory line in races at the Circus and to whiten the feet of imported slaves at
auctions. [Pliny the Elder, *Natural History* XXXV, 199]

Those from the East often had their ears pierced.

The slave auctions, like all markets, were supervised by state
officials. There were a number of regulations about the sale of slaves.
Each one had to wear a placard round his neck and the dealer was
bound to list the slave's faults and state his nationality. One
regulation contained the following instruction to slave-dealers:

Every slave's placard must be written in such a way that the customer can clearly understand what disease or defect each one has and which one is a runaway slave. [Aulus Gellius, IV 2.1]

Slaves of great beauty or value were not displayed publicly but were shown to buyers in private.

Evidence from Egypt shows that there was an official contract of sale. This included the approximate age of the slave and a list of his or her physical markings, presumably for identification purposes.

PRICES OF SLAVES

It is very difficult to give more than a general guide to the prices of slaves in Rome. Those that we have are spread over a period of centuries. Even when we have two prices from the same period we often are not told what special skills or qualities the slaves possessed. In general the cost varied according to a slave's appearance, training or novelty value. Female slaves, unless attractive, were cheaper than male ones.

It is also difficult to establish the value of Roman money. We cannot say how many pence a sestertius or denarius was worth. In looking at the price of slaves we can only judge one slave against another and perhaps compare their value with the following:

to be a senator it was necessary to have at least 1,000,000 sesterces (in cash or land)

to be a knight it was necessary to have at least 400,000 sesterces (in cash or land)

an ordinary soldier in the late Republic received 900 sesterces a year

an unskilled worker might earn about 1,000 sesterces a year

However, since Roman society used money far less than we do, these comparisons must be tentative.

In the time of Horace an ordinary slave could be bought for 2,000 sesterces whereas a clever, home-bred slave who had been trained as a reader fetched 8,000 sesterces. Columella later suggests that the same price should be paid for a skilled vine-dresser.

The following table gives a range of items:

Sesterces	Item	Date
100,000 each	for 11 slaves, each could recite the work of a Greek poet	before 65 A D
4,800	a male slave	first century A D

TO BE SOLD OR LET

BY PUBLIC AUCTION

On Monday the 18th of MAY, 1829.

UNDER THE TREES.

FOR SALE

THE THREE FOLLOWING

SLAVES

VIZ.

HANNIBAL, about 30 Years old, an excellent House Servant and of Good
WILLIAM, about 35 Years old, a Labourer.   [Character
NANCY, an excellent House Servant and Nurse.

The MEN belonging to "LEECH'S" Estate, and the WOMAN to Mrs. D. SMITH.

TO BE LET

On the usual conditions of the Hirer finding them in Food, Clothing & Medical Attendance.

THE FOLLOWING

MALE AND FEMALE

SLAVES

OF GOOD CHARACTERS.

ROBERT BAGLEY, about 20 Years old, a good House Servant.
WILLIAM BAGLEY, about 18 Years old, a Labourer.
JOHN ARMS, about 18 Years old.
JACK ANTONIA, about 40 Years old, a Labourer.
PHILIP, an Excellent Fisherman.
HARRY, about 27 Years old, a good House Servant.
LUCY, a Young Woman of good Character, used to House Work
ELIZA, an Excellent Washerwoman.   [and the Nursery.
CLARA, an Excellent Washerwoman.
FANNY, about 14 Years old, House Servant.
SARAH, about 14 Years old, House Servant.

ALSO FOR SALE AT ELEVEN O'CLOCK.

FINE RICE, GRAIN, PADDY, BOOKS, MUSLINS, NEEDLES, PINS,

RIBBONS, &c., &c.

AT ONE O'CLOCK, THAT CELEBRATED ENGLISH HORSE

BLUCHER.

34040

3   A nineteenth-century American slave-sale notice

Sesterces	Item	Date
4,050	a male slave at Herculaneum	63 AD
2,700	a cook	before 80 AD
1,200	a female slave, aged 25	129 AD
900	a male slave at Herculaneum	before 80 AD
725 each	two boys at Pompeii	61 AD
640	a girl aged 8 in Egypt	77 AD

In the late Republic and early Empire the prices for unusual or gifted slaves reached amazing heights. Ethiopian slaves, for instance, were highly valued. So were dwarfs. The dwarfs were usually misshapen and half-witted, with bald, pointed heads and long ears. It was considered fashionable to keep dwarfs in order to provide amusement; often as a joke they were given the names of mighty Greek warriors such as Achilles and Agamemnon. The Emperor Augustus detested dwarfs but his wife Livia, along with many other great ladies in Rome, delighted in them. The satirical poet Martial in a couple of short poems pokes fun at the fashion:

If you only saw his head you would think it was Hector. But if you saw him standing you would think it was Astyanax! (Hector's baby son)
[Martial, XIV 212]

and he mentions a notorious slave-dealer of his day, Gargilianus:

You told me he was an idiot, so I bought him for 20,000 sesterces. Give me back my money, Gargilianus; he is quite sane! [Martial, VIII 13]

We have already had occasion to quote Pliny the Elder, whose *Natural History* is a cross between an encyclopaedia and the *Guinness Book of Records*. Pliny gives the following figures which, if they are not absolutely reliable, do at least serve as an indication of the sort of prices that could be paid:

The highest price paid for a person born in slavery was, as far as I have been able to find out, for a skilled linguist called Daphnis. Marcus Scaurus bid 700,000 sesterces for him. In our own time actors have paid far more than this to buy their freedom with their earnings.
... Clutorius Priscus bought Paezon, one of Sejanus' eunuchs, for 50,000,000 sesterces. [*Natural History* VII 128–9]

Pliny also gives an anecdote about the notorious slave-dealer

Toranius who was doing business in the time of Mark Antony and Octavian. The story illustrates the search for novel slaves, the trickery and glib tongue of the dealer, and the price that could be paid.

The slave-dealer Toranius sold Mark Antony two very handsome boys. Though one was born in Asia and the other came from somewhere north of the Alps, the dealer sold them as twins for they were so much alike. Later when the boys' speech revealed the fraud, Antony angrily protested to the dealer. He complained especially about the large price – 200,000 sesterces. The crafty dealer replied that the difference in race was precisely the reason why he had charged so much. He said there was nothing unusual in twins looking alike, but, he added, to find boys of different races so alike in appearance was beyond all price. [*Natural History* VII 56]

Antony was delighted!
   But not all slave-dealers were quite so successful in persuading their audiences:

A girl of doubtful reputation, one of the sort who sit in the middle of the Subura[1], was recently being sold by the auctioneer Gellianus. Since for some time the bidding had been slow, he wanted to prove to his audience that she was quite healthy. So he pulled the girl to him, though she was reluctant, and gave her two, three, four kisses. Do you want to know what he achieved by this? He kissed good-bye to 600 sesterces – the bidder *withdrew* his offer!
[Martial, VI 66]

Numbers of slaves

As with the price of slaves, our evidence here is thin and there is great dispute amongst scholars over the interpretation of it; but ancient historians mention figures which suggest that the number of slaves in Italy at the start of the second century BC could have been as high as 500,000. It is possible that at the time of the Emperor Augustus the number may have been as high as 3,000,000 out of a population of about 7,500,000.

SLAVES OWNED BY THE RICH

Most of these slaves were employed on the land on the estates of rich

1   The Subura was a busy and noisy quarter north of the forum in Rome. It was filled with shops and workshops and was in many ways like the district of Soho in London.

landowners. There are no reliable figures for the size of such estates or for the number of slaves employed. Cato had suggested for an oliveyard of about 70 hectares that there should be 13 slaves consisting of an overseer, a housekeeper, 5 labourers, 3 ploughmen, a mule-handler, a swineherd and a shepherd. For a vineyard of 30 hectares he suggested 15 slaves: an overseer, a housekeeper, 10 labourers, a ploughman, a mule-handler and a swineherd. A villa that has been excavated near Pompeii seems to support these numbers. Its landholdings were about 80 hectares, and the main concentration on its vineyards. The slave quarters had had room for about 30 slaves. The Elder Pliny, however, records an outstanding case:

In 8 BC Gaius Caecilius Isidorus, a freedman of Gaius Caecilius, made a will in which he declared that, although he had suffered heavy losses in the civil war, he still left 4,116 slaves, 3,600 pairs of oxen, 257,000 other cattle, and 60,000,000 sesterces. He also gave instructions that 1,100,000 sesterces should be spent on his funeral.

[Pliny the Elder, *Natural History* XXXIII 135]

Petronius deliberately exaggerates his description of Trimalchio's estates when he records that 70 slaves were born on one day and further emphasises Trimalchio's wealth by comparing his slaves to an army with its various units:

Trimalchio then said to the cook in a loud voice: 'Which division of slaves are you from?'
When the cook replied that he was from the fortieth division, Trimalchio asked: 'Were you bought or were you born here?' 'Neither,' said the cook, 'I was left to you by Pansa in his will.'
'Well,' said Trimalchio, 'make sure that you serve it up carefully – or I'll have you demoted to the messenger division!' [Petronius, *Satyricon* 47]

Once again Petronius is obviously exaggerating and some would say that his description has no connexion with real life. But it does not seem unreasonable to suggest that a wealthy Roman might possess over 400 slaves in his household and on his estates. In the first century BC Marcus Crassus the Triumvir had formed his own fire brigade of 500 slaves and possessed many more in his household. Tacitus records that in AD 61 Pedanius Secundus, the Prefect of the City of Rome, was murdered by one of his slaves. According to law all the slaves who lived under the same roof had to be executed. These numbered 400, but he probably had many others on his estate to provide him with his wealth.

Pliny the Elder contrasts the 'legions of slaves' of his day with the past 'when there was one slave for each master'. Certainly among the rich and fashionable Romans the possession of slaves was an indication of status:

The first question about a person concerns his wealth. 'How many slaves has he got? How much land? What's the value of his dinner service?'

[Juvenal, *Satires* III 140–42]

The Emperor Augustus in AD 12 restricted to 20 the number of slaves that a man who was exiled could take with him. He also restricted the number of slaves that a man could set free in his will. The regulations cover people who owned from 1 to over 500 slaves. Pliny the Younger seems to have manumitted 100 in his will. If this is the case, then he must have had at least 500 slaves (see p. 69).

But the majority of people who owned slaves must have had far fewer than this number. The poet Horace says:

My supper is served by three slaves.

and warns one of his household slaves:

If you don't take yourself off smartish, you'll become the ninth labourer on my Sabine estate!

Of one character, whose behaviour went to extremes, he comments:

Often he would keep 200 slaves, often only 10.

while of the praetor Tillius he says:

No-one will taunt me with meanness, as he does you, when only 5 slaves accompany you on the road to Tibur.

[Horace, *Satires* I 6, II 7, I 3, I 6]

From the excavations at the port of the Ostia, at the mouth of the Tiber, it seems that a slave household of 20 should be considered large.

We cannot say for certain at what level of society people became too poor to own *any* slaves, but tombstones in the poorer part of the cemetery at Ostia do mention that they are for the person's freedmen as well. If a person could afford a tombstone, he most likely had at least one slave. That there were some Romans who could not afford even one slave is certain. The down-and-outs who slept under the bridges could scarcely afford a crust of bread. The blocks of flats also contained many poor people who were out of work, or casual labourers who relied heavily on their patron's handouts. Juvenal mentions the poet Cordus who had a wife, a bed, six mugs, a sideboard, a jug, a small statue and a chest of books which the mice ate. Such people as this had no slaves.

Juvenal when describing a drunk who is looking for a fight shows the difference in the man's behaviour towards the rich man who has a bodyguard of slaves and the poor man on his own.

He's wise enough to keep out of the way of the man with the scarlet cloak and his large following of clients and slaves, the mass of torches and the bronze lantern that shows his wealth and power. But as for me, as I make my way home by the light of the moon or the tiny light of a candle, carefully trimming the wick to make it last, he knows that I'm easy meat.

[Juvenal, *Satires* III 283–8]

4

The treatment of slaves and their occupations

To the Romans, a slave was a *res*, an object, a piece of property. He could be bought, sold, and left in a will. If a person injured someone else's slave, that person could be sued for damages in a court of law. The charge was not that he had injured the slave but that he had damaged the owner's property. The early view of slaves was that, along with worn-out cattle and ploughs, they were implements to be sold when no longer useful. The Romans did not believe that slavery was wrong: it was universal practice at this time. As we have already said, they shared the belief, common in the ancient world, that other races were inferior to one's own and could be considered as born for slavery.

The slave had no civil status or rights. He could not own any property, he could not vote or serve in the army. He could not legally marry but he could with his master's permission enter into a 'form of marriage' (*contubernium*). He could not bring an action in a law court, and if he was required to answer questions in a law court, his evidence was only allowed if it had been obtained under torture (see p. 55).

Slaves formed part of their owner's household (*familia*). The head of the household (*paterfamilias*) had complete control over them. He could punish them by whipping them, imprisoning them in a slave prison (*ergastulum*), or even by having them executed (see p. 30). However, under the Empire several laws were passed limiting a master's rights and improving the position of slaves (see chapter 5).

We shall now look in detail at the occupation of slaves and the way they were treated.

Slaves on a villa rustica

Most of our information on the treatment of farm slaves comes from three writers of handbooks on agriculture: Cato (234–149 BC), Varro

(116–27 BC) and Columella (writing about AD 60). The fact that they did not write at the same time makes it dangerous to draw any general conclusions about farm-slaves at one particular time, but it does help to show that attitudes towards slaves varied at different periods.

The large proportion of slaves in Italy were employed on farms or country estates (*villae rusticae*). The owners of these did not usually live on the estate but left its management to a bailiff (*vilicus*). Since an owner had little or no contact with his slaves the latter's chances of earning their freedom were greatly reduced.

A slave was part of the farm property, a living tool, and was classed along with the farm stock. The Elder Cato urges:

Look over your livestock and hold a sale ... Sell any oxen that are too old to be of use. Sell your inferior cows and sheep, wool, skins, an old wagon, old tools, an old slave, a sick slave and anything else that is no longer of use.

[Cato, *On Agriculture* 2.7]

Farms were investments and had to make a profit, and the treatment of the slave workers was based on this fact. Here is Cato again:

From the prisoners taken in war Cato bought many slaves – especially those who were young and could still be reared and trained like whelps and colts ... At home the slave had either to perform his job or be asleep. Cato particularly liked the sleepy ones as they were easier to handle; he thought too that after sleep they were better able to cope with a job than those who were less interested in their beds.

Later, when he grew richer and entertained his friends and fellow officials at dinner, he used, as soon as the meal was over, to punish with a whip the ones who had been careless in preparing or serving it. He made sure that his slaves always disagreed amongst themselves as he was suspicious and afraid of them when they were united. It was a rule of his that slaves charged with an offence deserving the death penalty should be judged by the whole slave household and should be put to death, if they were found guilty.

[Plutarch, *Cato the Elder* 21]

LIFE ON A FARM

Life on a farm was harder in general for a slave than life in the city. He had a longer day – nine to fifteen hours with a break in the middle. Every nine days there was a market day but there were no regular breaks to look forward to such as our weekend. Holidays on the farm were less frequent than in the city; and we cannot be sure how many days' holiday a slave received. Columella states:

45 days are allowed for wet weather and holidays. Similarly, after the sowing is completed, 30 days are allowed for rest.

[Columella, *On Agriculture* 2.12.9]

In Cato's day there seem to have been fewer holidays:

In bad weather, when the outdoor work can't be done, give the ox-stalls and sheep-pen a good clean or mend wine jars. Remember that if nothing is done the expenses still mount up. [Cato, *On Agriculture* 39]

Although he instructed his bailiff to observe feast days, he suggests there was work even then:

You may yoke oxen on feast days. These are the jobs they may do: pulling firewood, bean-stalks and grain for storage. There is no holiday for mules or donkeys except during the family festivals. [Cato, *On Agriculture* 138]

Presumably the oxen, mules and donkeys needed handlers. Cato was a hard task-master and control on his estates was strict. Varro shows a more humane attitude:

You should win the good will of the foremen by treating them with consideration. As for workers who outshine the others, you should discuss with them also what work is to be done. If you do this, they are less likely to think that they are looked down on but rather that they are valued by their master. They will do better work with more generous treatment: for example, extra food or clothing, or exemption from work, or permission to graze some cattle on the farm, or a similar bonus. The result is that if they are given some extra heavy work or punishment, the knowledge of their master's generosity will help to retain their good will and loyalty.

[Varro, *On Agriculture* 1.17]

So does Columella:

With regard to the other slaves, these are the general rules to be followed and I don't regret having kept to them myself: to talk on familiar terms with country slaves more often than with town ones – provided they have not behaved out of turn ... I now often consult them over a new project, crediting them with more experience, and this helps me to discover each one's capabilities and intelligence. [Columella, *On Agriculture* 1.8.15]

The *vilicus* himself was generally a slave. In his master's absence he had complete control over the slaves and even over free labourers that might be employed at busy times such as the harvest. The ancient writers listed the duties of a bailiff and advised owners how to choose one. Cato states:

He must settle any disagreements that may arise between slaves, and if one of them does something wrong, he must punish him according to his offence. It's his job to see that the slave household is provided for and that they do not suffer from cold or hunger ... He must show that he is grateful for good work so that others will work well ... He must keep the slaves busy and make sure that his master's instructions are carried out.

[Cato, *On Agriculture* 5]

Columella's advice is:

Don't choose a bailiff from slaves who have previously been working in the city and have got used to the circus, the theatres, gambling and taverns – their minds are preoccupied with these pleasures and so slaves, master and estates all suffer as a result of their idleness. Choose a man who has been hardened by farm work from his childhood, a man of experience. He should be middle-aged, strong, painstaking and skilled in farming. It doesn't matter if he is illiterate provided he can remember things. In fact he will be less likely to swindle his master if he can't read and write. He should be given a wife who can be a positive help to him. [Columella, *On Agriculture* 1.8]

MEDICAL TREATMENT

Farm slaves, it seems, were at least adequately fed and clothed. They were also kept in reasonable health. Cato mentions various treatments for sprains, swellings and wounds. He also has some violent-sounding purges for stomach-ache – the sort of minor complaint that a lazy slave might invent to get off work. One purge was made by boiling together some ham, cabbage leaves, fern, mussels, a fish, one scorpion, six snails and a handful of lentils. Columella talks of a hospital and says that in the event of injury the bailiff should:

apply poultices, or take the slave to the infirmary at once and give instructions for the use of any treatment that is necessary.

[Columella, *On Agriculture* 11.1.18]

Most Roman farms had a prison (*ergastulum*) where slaves were kept in chains overnight. The inmates were slaves who had displeased their master or bailiff. Columella gives the following advice on how to run a prison:

A careful master should inspect the slaves in the prison to find out whether they are securely chained, whether the prison buildings themselves are sufficiently safe and secure, and whether the bailiff has put any slave in chains or released him without orders ... The owner should take particular care in his inspection to see that such slaves are not being unjustly treated in matters of clothing and other allowances. For since they are controlled by several people – bailiff, foreman, jailer – they are more exposed to unfair treatment. They are also more dangerous if they are provoked by the cruelty and greed of their overseers. A sensible master, therefore, asks whether they are receiving the allowances due to them according to his instructions. He also tests the quality of their food and drink by tasting it himself and examines their clothing, gloves and footwear. [Columella, *On Agriculture* 1.8.16]

4   *A slave-chain with six collars, discovered near Cambridge*

The prisons were usually situated underground and were supervised by a trusted slave:

The chained workers should have an underground prison. It should be as healthy as possible and lit by several narrow windows high enough from the ground to be out of reach. [Columella, *On Agriculture* 1.6.3]

At a villa near Pompeii the prison included a set of stocks in which seven prisoners could be locked together by their feet.

The use of chained labour persisted into the second century A D at least. Martial writing at the turn of the century says:

Let the fields of Tuscany ring with the sound of countless chains.

[Martial, IX 22.4]

Columella, for all his reasonable advice on the treatment of chained labour, looked on the prison as a normal part of the farm. Other writers condemn this practice:

It is disgusting that the countryside should be farmed by prison gangs of slaves. [Pliny the Elder, *Natural History* XVIII 7]

The philosopher Seneca (c. 4 B C–A D 65) remarks:

It's strange that we should think it a good thing to send a poor unfortunate slave to prison. Why are we so anxious to beat him at once and break his legs? We should wait until our anger has cooled off before fixing a punishment. For we punish by sword and execution, chains, imprisonment and starvation a crime that deserves only a light beating.

[Seneca, *On Anger* III 32]

While, however, recommending humane treatment, Seneca gives some possible reasons why a slave might be punished:

If a prisoner of war suddenly thrown into slavery keeps some traces of freedom and doesn't jump at the idea of performing some degrading and laborious task; if he is slow because he is unfit and doesn't keep up with the speed of his master's carriage; if in the midst of his daily duty he falls asleep; if after being transferred from the city with its holidays to the farm with its hard work, he either refuses the work on the farm or doesn't tackle it energetically – in all these cases we should find out whether the slave cannot do the work or simply will not do it. [Seneca, *On Anger* III 29]

The Emperor Augustus ordered the prisons to be investigated and Hadrian tried to abolish them, but without complete success.

REWARDS FOR FARM SLAVES

Columella mentions freeing some slaves. What were a farm slave's chances of gaining his freedom? Since, as we have seen, he had little or no contact with his master, he was unlikely to impress him with his work or to bring himself to his master's attention by some outstanding service. City slaves were often given sums of money (*peculium*) which they could save to buy their freedom – if their master agreed. This idea was rarer with farm slaves. The more regular rewards were promotion – to bailiff or foreman – and the granting of privileges such as extra food and clothing. These rewards were also more useful. Farming was the only trade they knew and casual work was hard to get and poorly paid in the Republic. So there seems to have been little point in freeing farm slaves. At least such a slave knew where his next meal was coming from.

What happened to the slaves when they became too old to work? In Cato's day they were sold off but we are not told who bought them (see p. 27). As conditions improved it seems probable that they stayed on at the estate, making do as best they could.

On a villa urbana

The *villa urbana* was a wealthy Roman's country house to which he went when he wanted to get away from the city. Cicero had one at Tusculum, one at Formiae, one at Antium and three on the bay of Naples (including one at Pompeii). Pliny the Younger had villas at Comum, Laurentum and in Tuscany.

Besides a maintenance staff at these villas the owner would use his regular household, bringing with him those that he needed for his comfort or his work. All were under his supervision and their conditions of work were more like those of city slaves.

Pliny, when describing his villa at Laurentum, shows his consideration for his slaves:

The rest of this wing is reserved for the use of my slaves and freedmen, but most of the rooms are elegant enough to house guests ... At the end of the terrace is a suite of rooms. When I am there I feel that I have got away from the rest of the house. I like this feeling, especially at the feast of the *Saturnalia*, when the rest of the house is filled with the sound of festivity. For in this way I don't disturb my slaves' enjoyment and they don't interrupt my work.

[Pliny the Younger, Letters II 17]

Pliny's slaves were rather lucky in the accommodation they received. Normal quarters were in the cramped upper stories of houses. Sometimes city slaves were even boarded out in dormitories.

But not every slave had a happy time at a *villa urbana*. It was in such a villa at Formiae that Larcius Macedo was viciously murdered by his slaves because of his cruelty (see p. 47).

In the mines

Most of our information on mining comes from Diodorus the Sicilian who wrote between 60 and 30 BC:

Later, when the Romans had conquered Spain, many Italians flocked to the mines and in their greed carried away great wealth. They purchased a large number of slaves and handed them over to the managers of the mining works. These men open up shafts in many areas and dig deep into the earth looking for the veins that are rich in silver or gold. They not only go down a great distance but also extend their shafts for many hundreds of metres, and build galleries off at an angle and in all directions. This is the way they mine the ore which provides them with their profits.

The slaves who work in the mines bring their masters vast and incredible profits, but at the same time they wear out their bodies working underground both day and night in the shafts. Many of them die because of the awful hardships they have to face. There is no stopping or break in their work. They are forced by the blows of their overseers to endure their terrible fate and they exhaust their life in this wretched way. Yet some of them, because of their physical and mental strength, manage to last out and endure their misery for a long time. Death is preferable to them because of the extent of their suffering. [Diodorus the Sicilian, 5.36,38]

In Egypt the slaves were chained and worked day and night. Pliny the Elder says that the same was true in Spain where mining was done by lamplight and miners did not see daylight for many months. Moreover there was the constant danger of the roof caving in and of the workers being crushed. For some this was perhaps a blessing. Strabo, describing a mine in Pontus, says:

Mt Sandaracurgium is a honeycomb of mines. *Publicani* (tax-farmers) used to work this mine. They used as miners the slaves who had been sold in the market place because of their crimes. Apart from the hard work involved, the air is deadly because of the oppressive smell of the ore and as a result the miners face an early death. Moreover, the mine is often idle because of the lack of profit, since it not only needs a work force of over 200 but also requires continuous replacements as the miners are exhausted by disease or die. [Strabo, 12.3.40]

The traditional labour force used in the mines consisted of prisoners of war and enslaved convicts. The prisoners of war were for the most part the dregs of the market. They had no skills and so could not be used for better jobs. They were bought in bulk to be worked to death and then replaced as cheaply as possible. The quotation from Strabo shows that even so, some mines were rather too expensive in manpower.

Most prisoners naturally died in the mines. No mention is made of official release except through the emperor's intervention in special cases. But occasionally officials made mistakes, and while Pliny was governing the province of Bithynia he faced the following problem:

In many cities and particularly Nicomedia and Nicaea there can be found people who have been condemned to the mines or to the arena or to punishments of a similar nature. But these people are now performing the duties of public slaves and are receiving regular annual payments for their food.

Trajan's answer shows the official view:

You must put this situation right. Prisoners condemned to the mines have not only been released without authority, as you state in your letter, but have also been given back their status as honest officials. Those who were sentenced less than ten years ago and were set free without authority should be returned to the mines. If there are any older men who were sentenced more than ten years ago, they should be assigned to those duties which are similar to penal slavery, such as cleaning the public baths and sewers or repairing the streets and roads. [Pliny the Younger, *Letters* X 31 & 32]

In the arena

Like the mine workers, gladiators were generally either war-captives

5 Gladiators, from a mosaic in the Galleria Borghese, Rome

or condemned criminals. After the capture of Jerusalem in AD 70, Titus left the disposal of the prisoners to his friend Fronto:

He chose for his triumphal procession the tallest and most handsome of the younger prisoners. Of the remainder, those over 17 years of age were either chained and sent to labour in the mines of Egypt, or were assigned to the provinces of Asia Minor to die in the amphitheatres, slaughtered by the sword or torn to pieces by wild beasts. Those under 17 were sold.

[Josephus, *The Jewish War* VI 9]

Some of the captives did not last long in the arena; but others were chosen for their strength, and, after training, might if they were lucky earn their freedom. Criminals faced various penalties: some were condemned to the sword (*ad gladium*), sentenced to die within a year; some were sent to the training school (*ad ludum*) and might, if they lived, be discharged after three years. Others, such as Androcles, were condemned to be thrown to the wild beasts (*ad bestias*). Seneca while writing of the vicious behaviour of the crowds at an arena, questions a spectator:

'But he was a robber and murdered someone!'
'What of it?' I replied. '*He* deserved to suffer this fate because he was a murderer. What have you done, my poor fellow, to deserve having to watch this sort of thing?' [Seneca, *Letters* VII 5]

GLADIATORIAL SCHOOLS

These slaves were kept and trained in gladiatorial schools owned either by private individuals or by the emperor. (Spartacus belonged to the school of Lentulus Batiatus at Capua.) Many were trained at Ravenna because it was a healthy spot, and there was a school at Pompeii. Whilst in the schools they were under the supervision of a trainer (*lanista*) who was usually an ex-gladiator himself. They were forced to train hard in preparation for their public appearances at which there was always the prospect of having to kill their opponent or be killed themselves. They did, however, receive nourishing food with a staple diet of barley and beans. Medical attention was also provided. Galen, the famous medical writer and anatomist, began his career as a doctor in a training school in Asia Minor where he had an excellent opportunity to study the treatment of wounds and to practise dissection on the bodies of dead gladiators.

Gladiators were housed in barracks and kept under strict guard. There were severe penalties for desertion, and floggings and the chains were regular punishments. The corpses of six chained prisoners were found in the barracks at Pompeii.

The fate of most gladiators was not a pretty one, but some who were successful and pleased the crowds gained great popularity – both for themselves and for their owners. They could earn their 'wooden sword' and freedom – and perhaps become trainers. A few even fought on voluntarily such as one Publius Ostorius at Pompeii who won 51 victories. For such men there were the privileges, favour and wealth that modern singers, sportsmen and film stars enjoy. An inscription in Pompeii records that Celadus, a gladiator who fought as a Thracian, was known as 'the heart-throb of the girls'; and during the eruption of Vesuvius a wealthy woman died whilst visiting the gladiators' barracks.

Gladiators could be bought and sold just like any other slave. They were expensive animals. They were bought as bodyguards, thugs or just as something fashionable to have about the house.

6 *Condemned criminals in the arena*

In the town

The Romans never developed industries on the modern scale, but there were many workshops and factories where slaves were employed on various forms of mass-production. These included brick-works, lamp-factories, lead-pipe works, glass-works and potteries. The largest single workshop mentioned by Pliny the Elder employed fifty-eight slaves.

TRIMALCHIO AGAIN

Much of the information we have about the occupations of slaves in the household comes from Petronius' novel, the *Satyricon*. In the section of the book where he describes Trimalchio's famous banquet we see his slaves at work:

Finally we took our places. Boys from Alexandria poured iced water over our hands. Others attended to our feet, removing our hangnails with great skill . . .
. . . Two long-haired Ethiopians followed, carrying small skin bottles like those used for scattering sand in the circus, and poured wine over our hands; after this point no-one offered us water. Our host was complimented on these elegant arrangements.

And very elegant they were. Of course this is pure satire on Petronius' part, but some of Trimalchio's ideas must have been shared by Petronius' fellow-Romans. Notice how Trimalchio refers to his slaves at the start of the meal:

I gave orders for each guest to have his own table. Then these smelly slaves won't crowd us as much.

Later when the wine and the food have had their effect, he becomes more tolerant:

My dears, slaves are human beings too. They drink the same milk as anybody else, even though luck's been against them. Still if nothing happens to me, they'll have their taste of freedom soon. In fact, I'm setting them all free in my will. I'm giving Philargyrus a farm and, what's more, the woman he lives with. As for Cario, I'm leaving him a block of flats, his five per cent manumission tax and a bed with all the trimmings.

7   *Slaves attending guests at a dinner party, from a wallpainting at Pompeii*

Apart from serving at table, slaves were employed in Trimalchio's household as dancers, musicians, doctors, chefs, meat-carvers, stewards – and even as a human calendar:

He has a clock in the dining room and a trumpeter to tell him how much longer he's got to live.

[Petronius, *Satyricon* 31, 34, 71]

ORDINARY HOUSEHOLD DUTIES

Most Roman households were not arranged on so grand a scale and slaves were employed to carry out the more usual domestic duties of cleaning, cooking, serving and gardening, while a well-educated slave had charge of the household accounts and acted as secretary to his master. A family with children also employed slaves as nurses and tutors:

39

Above all, see that the child's nurse speaks correctly ... No doubt the most important point is that she should be of good character, but she should speak correctly as well ... As regards the paedagogus (child's tutor), I would urge in addition that he should have had a thorough education.

[Quintillian, *Education of the Orator* I 1.4–11]

But this ideal picture of the care of a young Roman was not often the reality as Tacitus tells us:

Nowadays we entrust the child to any little Greek slave girl, with one or another of the male slaves to help her – usually the most worthless of the whole household, utterly unfit for any serious service. Tender and impressionable minds are filled from the very start with these slaves' stories and prejudices, and no-one in the whole house cares a damn what he says or does in the presence of his infant master. [Tacitus, *Dialogue on Oratory* 29]

AN EASIER LIFE

The work of a town slave was in general easier than that of an agricultural slave. The slaves in the workshops, on building sites and in the bakeries no doubt did work hard but they enjoyed a larger number of holidays and worked fewer hours. According to their skill, they could earn promotion, and even their freedom. The household slaves also worked fewer hours even though they might be on call twenty-four hours a day to attend to their master's wishes. Moreover, since many of the slaves were specialists such as litter-bearers, readers and hairdressers, they did not work all the time but were busy for short periods. Again, much depended on the slave's value and importance and on the attitude of individual masters. A trained, reliable accountant, who was hard to replace, would naturally receive better treatment than a mere odd-job man or serving-girl. Pliny showed consideration for all his slaves, but he went to great lengths to send a favourite reader of his on a holiday to convalesce after an illness (see p. 54).

PECULIUM

Unlike the agricultural slaves, many, if not most, of the town slaves were given a wage (*peculium*) by their master. Legally, since a slave could not own anything, it remained the property of his master.

8   A slave out shopping

However, slaves were usually allowed to save up their *peculium* in order to purchase their freedom (see chapter 7). In addition, public slaves had the privilege of being able to dispose of half of it in their will, while Pliny permitted his slaves to dispose of it within the household when they were dying.

I let even those who remain slaves make a type of will which I treat as legally binding. They can set out their instructions and requests as they see fit, and I carry them out as if acting under their orders. They can distribute their possessions and make any bequests they like within the limits of the household: for the house provides the slave with a country and a form of citizenship. [Pliny the Younger, *Letters* VIII 16]

Other generous masters allowed similar privileges (see p. 66).

BURIAL

Many masters built tombs to contain the ashes of their slaves. The tomb set up by the Statilian family at Rome records amongst others this inscription:

Scaeva, a letter carrier of Statilius Taurus, erected this to his wife, Italia, a spinning maid. She lived 20 years. [Dessau, *ILS* 7432c]

The use of the word *wife* in this inscription must be an unofficial use allowed within the slave household: it shows that slaves could lead a reasonable family life if they had a tolerant master. In another example from Carthage, in North Africa, an ex-slave repaired his slave-parents' tomb:

To my most dutiful parents, Victor and Urbica, slaves of the emperor. Iucundus, freedman of the emperor, assistant in the judicial department, renovated this monument. Victor lived 102 years, Urbica 80 years.

[Dessau, *ILS* 1680]

The age of Iucundus' parents certainly indicates that slavery could be bearable.

But not all slaves were granted such honourable resting places. The slaves who possessed a skill could join guilds (*collegia*), which provided amongst other things a burial club. For the poorest slaves, however, burial was a very humble affair. Their ashes were placed in the ground and the neck of a wine jar was fixed over the spot. Through this, offerings could be poured to the gods.

Public slaves

The state and the towns, too, owned slaves. Many were used for small clerical jobs, especially in financial affairs. Others were storekeepers, keepers of records, temple caretakers and workers at the baths. They were also commonly employed as assistants to town officials or to the magistrates called *aediles* who looked after the maintenance of buildings, roads and sewers:

Marcus Agrippa also kept his own gang of slaves for the maintenance of the aqueducts, reservoirs and collection basins. Agrippa bequeathed this gang to the Emperor Augustus in his will and Augustus in turn left it to the state.

[Frontinus, *The Water Supply of Rome* 2.98]

At sacrifices public slaves assisted the priests and augurs. Like the slave craftsmen they would belong to a trade guild organisation (*collegium*) or they could organise their own. In these guilds they could

9 A relief from an altar at Pompeii, showing slaves assisting at a sacrifice

gain office and prestige and enjoy finally the benefits of the burial clubs.

THE EMPEROR'S SLAVES

The emperors also had their own body of slaves (*servi Caesaris*) to look after their private and official needs. Many were used for clerical jobs in the emperor's court and had slaves working under them. The chances of freedom were good, and for a few able and ambitious freedmen there were positions high up in the emperor's civil service which carried vast power and influence. But by far the great majority of the emperor's slaves were occupied in humble jobs around the palace such as footman, litter-bearer, wine steward, tailor, chamberlain, valet, overseer of furniture, overseer of lighting, slave in charge of jewellery, and so on.

43

5

Attitudes towards slaves

Much evidence exists from the late Republic and early Empire showing that while some masters displayed brutality and neglect towards their slaves, others acted in a kindly way and showed concern for their well-being. There was no sudden change of attitude on the part of masters during this period; indeed incidents related in our sources reveal examples of both kinds of behaviour. However, we can, perhaps, detect an overall change for the better from the time of Augustus onwards. One reason for this improvement has been mentioned already: the number of new slaves available from wars sharply declined with the advent of an era of peace that, broadly speaking, marked the end of Rome's territorial expansion. This meant that slaves were now expensive to replace. A reason of quite another kind was that the philosophical beliefs of Stoicism had grown fashionable – and one of these beliefs was that all men were equal. Although the Stoics did not take this idea too seriously, it did lead to the growth of a more humane attitude – as did the early Christian teachings. Another Stoic belief urged people to exercise self-control and act with moderation, and no doubt this, too, helped to make masters display more kindness towards their slaves. But, in general, throughout the period, simple common sense dictated that a master secured better and more productive work from his slaves if he treated them in a reasonable manner.

CICERO

The literary and personal writings of Cicero give us a good insight into his attitude towards his slaves and freedmen. Cicero, in common with his contemporaries, accepted slavery as part of the natural order of things:

Admittedly rulers who use force to hold down their subjects have sometimes to be cruel, as masters have to be towards slaves if they can find no other way to control them.

But he also comments in the same work:

Those who tell us to treat our slaves as we would our employees advise us well. Slaves must do their work; but they must also be given their due.

[Cicero, *On Duties* II 7, I 41]

TIRO

Cicero was a considerate man who believed that a slave's life would be intolerable if he were not offered some hope of freedom. Tiro was born a slave in the household of Cicero's father. He was an excellent example of the home-born slave (*verna*) who showed promise and was given the chance to realise this potential. Cicero had him educated, and trained him to be his private secretary and literary assistant. This naturally led to a close relationship, and in Cicero's letters we can see the sort of friendship that could exist between a master and a trusted slave or freedman. Writing to Tiro in 53 BC Cicero shows his concern:

Aegypta arrived to-day. Although he told me that you had got over the fever and were in good shape, he said that you had not been able to write to me. That worried me, particularly since Hermia, who should have arrived to-day, hasn't come. You just can't imagine how anxious I am about your health ... I'd write more if I thought you could now read with ease. Meanwhile apply that mind of yours, which I value so much, to the job of getting yourself well – for both our sakes. Take good care of yourself. Good-bye.

P.S. Hermia arrived just as I finished this and I have now received your letter. The handwriting's rather shaky but no wonder considering your condition. I've sent you Aegypta to keep you company. He's not uncultured and he seems very fond of you. I've also sent you a cook to use. Good-bye.

[Cicero, *Letters to friends* XVI 15]

Tiro was given his freedom shortly after this. Quintus Cicero who had freed one of his slaves named Statius a few years earlier wrote to his brother Marcus to congratulate him:

Dear Marcus, I'm delighted you thought Tiro worthy of his freedom and preferred to have him as a friend rather than a slave. Believe me, when I read your letter, I jumped for joy. Do accept my congratulations. For when I consider how much Statius' loyalty pleases me, I realise you must value Tiro very highly since he's not only loyal but also a cultured and literary man.

[Cicero, *Letters to friends* XVI 16]

In 50 BC Cicero returned from the province of Cilicia where he had been governor. Tiro's health had again been bad – from overwork – and he had to be left behind on the journey to recover. Cicero wrote to him:

I read your letter with mixed feelings. I was very disturbed by the first page, though somewhat reassured by the second. So now I'm even more convinced that you should not make the journey either by land or sea until you are completely recovered. It will be soon enough for me to see you if I see you well and strong again. As for your doctor, you say he is well thought of and that is what I hear too; but I really don't approve of his treatment. You shouldn't have been given soup when you had a bad stomach. However, I've written him a detailed letter ... One thing only, my dear Tiro, I beg of you: please don't spare any expense where your health is concerned. I have told Curius in my letter to let you have any money you ask for. The doctor should, I think, be given something in advance to make him take more interest. The help you have given me is immeasurable – at home and in my legal work, in Rome and in my province, in my private affairs and public life, in my reading and literary work. Yet the best gift you can give me is to come back perfectly fit again. [Cicero, *Letters to friends* XVI 4]

CAREERS FOR HOUSEHOLD SLAVES

Slaves like Tiro, who were trained in a household, sometimes had opportunities for an interesting career. This might bring them their freedom and, in some cases, great wealth often at an early age. In return, their masters had their services and the reputation that a learned household could bring. At the same time a handsome profit could be made from any expert slaves they sold. The range of skills such slaves could acquire was wide. Some were taught to be librarians, copyists, readers and grammarians; others were trained for practical jobs such as clerks, short-hand writers, linguists, accountants, doctors, writers and cooks.

The schoolmaster Lutatius Daphnis was purchased for 700,000 sesterces and was soon set free. The comic dramatist Publius Terentius Afer (Terence) had been a slave in Carthage and then in

Rome. Antonius Musa, a slave of Mark Antony or his family, became Augustus' doctor and built up a very profitable practice. Such notable ex-slaves received full recognition for their abilities in Roman society.

Here is an epitaph to a young accountant at Ostia:

To the Gods of the Underworld. This is the tomb of Melior, the accountant. He lived 13 years. His memory and learning were such that he surpassed on the tombstones the praises of all others, from past memory to the day of his death. The individual branches of learning that he knew could be written in a book rather than in an epitaph ... Sextus Aufustius Agreus, his most unfortunate teacher, set this up to his slave (*verna*). [Dessau, *ILS* 7755]

Another inscription records the death of a *verna* who had been set up in business at an inn:

Vitalis, the slave and son of Gaius Larius, born at his house, is buried here. He lived 16 years. He was the manager of the Taberna Apriana (near Philippi). He was accepted by the people but snatched away by the gods. I ask you, travellers, to forgive me for any short measure that I gave you in order to help my father. I ask you in the name of the gods both above and below to allow me to commend my mother and father to you.

[Dessau, *ILS* 7479]

LARCIUS MACEDO

It was also possible for the son of a man who had been a slave to make a good career for himself. Pliny mentions Larcius Macedo as an example. Macedo's father had been a slave but his son still attained one of the highest offices in Rome. Of course he was lucky but, as we shall see, he paid a penalty for his success. Macedo's story reveals the brutality of some masters and the fact that the laws concerning slaves were sometimes harsh.

It was a shocking fate (and it calls for something more than a letter) that Larcius Macedo, an ex-praetor, suffered at the hands of his own slaves. I admit that Macedo was an overbearing and altogether brutal master, who too easily forgot that his father had been a slave, or perhaps too readily remembered it.

He was bathing in his villa at Formiae when suddenly he was surrounded by his slaves. One made for his throat, another hit him in the face, while a third punched him in the chest and stomach and even, I'm afraid to say, in his private parts. When they thought he was dead they threw him out on to the hot floor to see whether he was still alive. Macedo was either unconscious or was pretending to be so. At any rate he lay stretched out and motionless and gave the impression that he was dead. Only then was he carried out as if he had been overcome with the heat. He was received by the slaves who had remained faithful to him, while his concubines rushed up to him shouting and screaming. Roused by their cries and brought round by the colder air he opened his eyes and, making some movement of his body, he showed that he was still alive – it was now safe to do so.

The other slaves fled. Most of them were caught and the rest are being looked for. Macedo was revived with difficulty and having survived a few days died, but not without the consolation of knowing that he had been avenged while still alive as only the murdered normally are.

[Pliny the Younger, *Letters* III 14]

The law decreed that all slaves living under their master's roof at the time of the murder should be put to death, regardless of whether they were guilty or not. No doubt they were considered to be so because they had failed to prevent the murder.

PEDANIUS SECUNDUS

In AD 61 Pedanius Secundus, Prefect of the city of Rome, was murdered by one of his slaves, either because the murderer had been refused his freedom or because he was his master's rival in a love affair. Tacitus tells what followed:

Ancient custom demanded that the whole slave household had to be executed. But a crowd gathered, anxious to save so many innocent people. There was almost a riot, and the senate-house was besieged. Among the senators themselves there were some opposed to excessive severity, but the majority were against any change. One of the latter was Gaius Cassius, who when his turn came to speak said: 'A former consul has been murdered by a slave in his own home. No-one prevented or betrayed him . . . If you want to exempt his fellow-slaves from the death-penalty, do so. But, remember, if the Prefect of the city was not protected by his position, who *is* going to be? No-one will feel safe, however many slaves he has, if Pedanius Secundus' four hundred were not enough. No-one is likely to get help from his slaves if they are not made to feel that if our lives are threatened, so too are theirs.

'It has even been argued that the murderer was avenging a wrong done to him. You might just as well say that he was justified in killing his master! . . .

'Do you believe that a slave can have planned to murder his master without letting slip one threatening or careless remark? All right, then, let us assume he kept his plan a secret, and got hold of a weapon without being noticed; but how could he have passed the guards, opened the bedroom door, carried in a light and committed the murder without anyone knowing? There are many warning signs of crimes. If slaves reveal them, we can live safely, although we are one among many, simply because they are concerned for their own safety. Or, if we must die, we shall not do so without the knowledge that the guilty will be punished.

'Our ancestors always regarded their slaves with suspicion – even when slaves were born on the same estates, or in the same homes, as their masters and had been kindly treated by them. But nowadays our households contain every nationality; they include every alien rite and belief – or, in some cases, none at all. The only way to control this rabble is to make them fear you. Innocent slaves will die, you say. Yes, they will ... Whenever people are punished as an example to others there is always an element of injustice. But the injustice to individuals is outweighed by the advantage to the community as a whole.'

No-one dared speak against Cassius, but protests were heard about the numbers involved, about the young children and women, and the fact that the majority of them were undoubtedly innocent. Yet those who favoured execution had their way. However, large crowds collected brandishing torches and stones and prevented the execution from being carried out. Nero issued a decree rebuking the populace, and lined with armed guards the entire route along which the condemned were led to execution.

[Tacitus, *Annals* XIV 42–5]

Pliny, who was in general a kind and trusting master expresses the same distrust of slaves as Cassius does when at the end of his story about Macedo he remarks:

You see the dangers, outrages and insults to which we are exposed. No master can feel secure because he is considerate and humane. Slaves murder their masters not on any rational grounds but from some brutal instinct.

[Pliny the Younger, *Letters* III 14]

Seneca records:

It was once proposed in the senate that slaves should be distinguished from free men by their dress; then we realised the danger we would be in if our slaves began to count us. [Seneca, *On Mercy* I 21.1]

The cruelty of some slave-owners gave them every right to be afraid. Here is Seneca again:

Could anyone have been more hated, even by his slaves, than Vedius Pollio? He fattened his man-eating fish on human blood, and ordered those who caused him any annoyance to be thrown into his fishpond, which was as deadly as a snake-pit. [Seneca, *On Mercy* I 18]

And this is Juvenal's description of a certain Rutilus:

Does Rutilus display a lenient temper and a sense of restraint when dealing with trivial faults? Does he hold that the bodies and souls of slaves are made of the same material and elements as our own? No, he does not! What he teaches is brutality: there's nothing he likes to hear more than the sound of a cruel flogging, no siren-song (he thinks) is sweeter. To his trembling household he is a complete monster, never happy until he has called for a torturer and some poor wretch is being branded with a hot iron – and all because of two missing towels. [Juvenal, *Satires* XIV 15 ff.]

No doubt Seneca and Juvenal are exaggerating, or at any rate quoting the worst cases, to prove their point. Seneca in fact tells us that cruel slave-owners like Pollio were treated with the utmost contempt in Rome. Martial satirises one such owner in this way:

You say that the hare is not cooked enough and shout for your whip. Clearly, Rufus, you prefer to cut up your cook than your hare. [Martial, III 94]

Such masters were exceptions. Town-slaves were, of course, punished when they did wrong. One can imagine cooks, slave-girl hairdressers and so on being very much in the firing line, but beatings were not the only form of punishment employed. Slaves might be demoted, lose their privileges, be given extra work, or, in severe cases, be sent to work on the estates. In the last resort, a master could have a slave killed (see also p. 56).

It is probably true that town-slaves had better reasons for behaving themselves than slaves on a big farm. The benefits of *peculium* and the eventual hope of freedom were not things to be lightly thrown away. We do not, for instance, hear of their joining in the great slave revolts, which are described in the next chapter. Where they were mistreated,

10   A lady at her toilet, attended by slave girls

they could run away – dangerous though that might have been for them. But, despite the cases of Macedo and Secundus, they were rarely a threat. Pliny may talk of the dangers owners faced from their slaves, but he says this, we must remember, in reaction to the murder of Macedo. There were likely to have been many owners who felt, on the contrary, that a slave deserved better treatment. And yet no one went so far as to condemn slavery outright, or to suggest that it should be abolished.

It is in the works of the same Seneca and Pliny (the Younger) from which we have been quoting that we can see a kinder and more considerate attitude being shown towards slaves during the early Empire.

Seneca writes:

To show restraint in controlling one's slaves is an admirable thing. Even when dealing with a human *possession* one should consider what is fair and just rather than how much the slave can endure without retaliating. Even prisoners and bought slaves deserve mercy ... Although when dealing with a *slave* the law imposes no restrictions, yet where a *human being* is involved there is a limit set by the law which applies to all living things.

[Seneca, *On Mercy* I 18]

SENECA'S HUMANITY

And in this longer and more notable passage from one of his letters the note of humanity is even more pronounced:

I am delighted to learn that you live on friendly terms with your slaves. This is in keeping with your common sense and learning. 'They are slaves', people say. No, they are men. 'Slaves!' No, comrades-in-arms. 'Slaves!' No, unassuming friends. 'Slaves!' No, they are our fellow-slaves, if one reflects that fortune rules over slaves and free men alike.

That's why I smile at those who think it degrading to dine with one's slave. Why do they think so? Because proud fashion decrees that a crowd of slaves shall stand around their master while he dines. He eats more than he can hold ... and the unfortunate slaves are not allowed to move their lips, even to speak. The slightest sound is checked with the rod; and even a chance cough, sneeze or hiccup is punished with the whip. The smallest breach of silence receives a severe penalty. All night long they stand around, hungry and dumb.

The outcome of this is that these slaves who may not talk in the presence of their master talk about him behind his back. But the slaves of former days, who were allowed to talk not only in their master's presence but actually with him, whose mouths were not sewn up tight, were prepared to bare their necks for their master and to bring down upon their own heads any danger that menaced him. They would speak at banquets but keep silent under torture. Finally there is a current saying about this same arrogant attitude: 'Every slave you own is a potential enemy.' They are not enemies when we obtain them, we make them enemies ...

Please remember that the man you call your slave was born of the same stock, sees the same skies, and breathes, lives, and dies, just like you. It is

just as possible for you to see him as a free man as it is for him to see you as a slave . . .

This is the gist of my advice: Treat your inferiors as you would want to be treated by your betters. And whenever you think of the control you have over your slave, remember that your master has as much control over you. 'But', you say, 'I have no master'. You are still young, and you may yet acquire one. Don't you know the age at which Hecuba became a captive slave . . . ?

Live with your slave on kindly, even on affable, terms: include him in your conversations, your plans, your life . . .

'He is a slave'. But perhaps he has the soul of a free man. 'He is a slave'. Is that to count against him? Point me out somebody who is not a slave. One man is a slave to his passions, another to his greed, another to ambition, and all men are slaves to fear. I will quote you a former consul who is slave to an old woman, a rich man who is slave to a chit of a maid-servant . . . No form of slavery is more degrading than that which we impose upon ourselves.

So there's no reason why you should be deterred by these snobbish people from showing yourself to your slaves as a good-humoured person instead of as arrogantly superior to them. They should respect you rather than fear you. Someone will say that I am now offering slaves the cap of freedom and pulling down masters from their pedestals because I have declared that slaves should respect rather than fear their masters . . . A person who is respected is loved, and love and fear cannot be mixed. So I consider you are doing quite the right thing in not wanting your slaves to fear you and in merely rebuking them with your tongue. Lashings with a whip are only for dumb animals. [Seneca, *Letters* XLVII]

Seneca appears to feel strongly about this matter, but his exceptionally generous view of a slave's position may have been influenced by what he thought it fashionable to write.

THE ATTITUDE OF PLINY

Pliny strikes a more personal but no less considerate note in his letters. When slaves and freedmen in his household are ill or die, he appears genuinely upset and writes in the most sympathetic terms about them:

I have been very distressed by illness amongst my slaves, and by the deaths also of some of the younger ones. Two things comfort me at a time like this, though needless to say not adequately: I am always prepared to give my slaves their freedom, for if they die as free men I don't feel their deaths are so untimely; and I let even those who remain slaves make a will which I regard as legally valid. [Pliny, *Letters* VIII 16]

So, upset as I am by my wife's poor health, the sickness in my household and the death of some of my slaves, I have immersed myself in my work, for this is the only way I can forget my worries. [Pliny, *Letters* VIII 19]

His letter about his freedman Zosimus is even more revealing:

Even if I were harsh and lacking in feeling, I would still be very distressed by the illness of my freedman Zosimus. He deserves kindness all the more now that he has so much need of it. He is honest, conscientious and educated, by profession, and according to his slave label, an actor – and a good one too. He recites clearly and intelligently and with the appropriate gestures; he also plays the lyre well – considerably better than is required of an actor. His reading of speeches, history and poetry is so good that he gives the impression of having devoted his whole training to this. I have spoken at length about him so that you may have a better idea of the many unique and delightful services I receive from him. Another reason is my longstanding affection for him which has grown with the dangers he has been through. For it appears a rule of nature that nothing arouses and stimulates love so much as the fear of losing what one loves, and this is something I have experienced more than once with him.

A few years ago, in the midst of a vigorous reading, he began to bring up blood. I sent him to Egypt, and after a long convalescence in that country he returned a little while ago quite fit again. Now after overstraining his voice for several days on end he has had another bout of coughing – a warning of his former illness; and once again he has started to spit blood. So I have made up my mind to send him to your estate at Forum Julii [modern Fréjus], for you have often told me that the air there is healthy and the local milk beneficial in complaints of this sort. Please write to your household there and ask them to welcome him on the estate and in your home, and to give him whatever money he needs. It won't be much because his wants are simple, and he goes not only without luxuries but even without things essential for his health. I will give him adequate travelling expenses this end for the journey to your estate. [Pliny, *Letters* V 19]

It is worthwhile comparing this with Cicero's letters to his freedman Tiro, quoted at the beginning of this chapter.

THE DEVOTION OF SLAVES TO THEIR MASTERS

Several outstanding examples also exist of the devotion of slaves towards their owners. A slave's evidence was only acceptable in a court of law if it had been obtained under torture. Cicero in one of his speeches well illustrates how loyal a slave could be:

The slaves were vigorously questioned under every form of torture. Although threats and promises were used to get them to say something ... they stuck to the truth and said they knew nothing ... The questioning was resumed ... The witnesses of the interrogation objected ... Sassia, that cruel and inhuman woman, flew into a rage because her plans were not going as she had hoped. Although the torturer and his instruments were now almost worn out, she still refused to stop. (The witnesses, however, decided that it had gone on long enough.) [Cicero, *For Cluentius* 63. 176]

Another example of such devotion is given by Tacitus:

On the next day the murder of Pontia was discovered. There was no doubt who the murderer was, for Pontia and Octavius were proved to have been together. Octavius' freedman, however, claimed that *he* had committed the murder. He said that he had done it to avenge the wrongs done to his former master by Pontia. Many were convinced by his devotion, but Pontia's slave-girl recovered from her wound and revealed the truth.

[Tacitus, *Annals* XIII 44]

In AD 62 Poppaea wanted to marry the Emperor Nero, but first she had to remove Nero's wife, Octavia:

Poppaea persuaded one of Octavia's servants to accuse Octavia of adultery. Eucaerus, a native of Alexandria and a skilled fluteplayer, was chosen for the part of her lover. Octavia's slave-girls were questioned. A few under the pressure of torture were induced to make false confessions but the majority persisted in stating that their mistress was innocent . . . Nonetheless, Octavia was divorced. [Tacitus, *Annals* XIV 60]

LEGISLATION IN FAVOUR OF SLAVES

Perhaps the most convincing evidence of an improvement in attitudes towards slaves during the early Empire can be seen in the laws passed on this subject under a number of emperors, in particular Claudius, Domitian and Hadrian.

Under Claudius:

Finding that several sick or worn-out slaves had been marooned by their owners on the island of Aesculapius in the river Tiber, to avoid giving them proper medical attention, Claudius freed them all and ruled that those who got well again should not return to their former owner. Furthermore, he decreed that any owner who, for the same sort of reason, abandoned a sick slave should henceforth be charged with murder. [Suetonius, *Claudius* 25]

Under Domitian:

Castration was now strictly prohibited and the price of eunuchs remaining in slave-dealers' hands officially controlled. [Suetonius, *Domitian* 7]

Under Hadrian:

Several laws relating to slavery were passed under Hadrian:
1   A restriction was placed on the use of torture for extracting information from slaves.
2   If a slave owner was murdered, only the slaves near the scene at the time were allowed to be questioned.
3   It was forbidden to sell a slave – without good reason – to a gladiatorial school or to a brothel.
4   A slave could no longer be killed by his master without the permission of a magistrate. (Antoninus Pius [AD 139–161]), made the owner answerable in law if he killed a slave.)
5   Slave-prisons (see chapter 4 above) were abolished.

6

Revolts

A likely cause of discontent and danger had always been the vast number of slaves employed, especially on the large estates. Three major slave revolts involving military campaigns took place during the Republic, two in Sicily (134–131 BC and 104–100 BC) and one in Italy itself (that of Spartacus in 73–71 BC). In view of the poor conditions on the estates, it is only surprising that there· were not more. Certainly the great majority of the slaves who took part in the uprisings came from these large estates.

REVOLTS IN SICILY

An account of the first revolt in Sicily is given by the historian Diodorus.

There never had been such an uprising of slaves as that which took place in Sicily [in 134 BC]. To most people the event came as a sudden and unexpected shock, but it did not occur for no reason. The fault lay in the rich land-owners who displayed both great wealth and great arrogance. Slaves were badly treated, and the more they were badly treated the more their hatred of their masters grew. At a convenient moment this hatred burst out into open revolt: slaves gathered in their thousands to destroy their masters ...

The uprising began as follows. Damophilus of Enna, in central Sicily, was one of the wealthy and arrogant land-owners we have mentioned above. He had purchased a large number of slaves and was treating them outrageously, branding men who in their own countries had been free but through capture in war were now slaves. Some of these he put in chains and thrust into slave-pens; others he appointed herdsmen but neglected to provide them with suitable clothing or food. His wife Megallis took equal pleasure in punishing her slave women.

The upshot was that the slaves began to plot their master's destruction, believing that they could not suffer a worse fate than their present one. Collecting four hundred of their fellow-slaves, and arming themselves as best they could, they burst into the town of Enna, entered houses and slaughtered many of the inhabitants. They even killed tiny babies, tearing them from their mother's breasts and throwing them to the ground.

The slaves chose Eunus, a Syrian magician, as their leader. Eunus at once ordered the execution of all the citizens of Enna with the exception of those who were skilled in manufacturing arms. After arming over 6,000 slaves he began to plunder the entire countryside, attracting as he did so an almost unlimited number of recruits. Confident enough, as a result, to fight the Roman army, he won battle after battle – thanks to his superior numbers, which by this time totalled 10,000. He was now joined by a Cilician named Cleon and the 5,000 slaves the latter brought with him. Together, their combined force was more than a match for the Roman general Lucius Hypsaeus who commanded a mere 8,000 Sicilian troops. This was the first of several victories won by Eunus and his slave rebels.

[Diodorus the Sicilian, XXXIV ff]

As the news of the revolt spread, uprisings occurred elsewhere. Approximately 1,000 slaves revolted, respectively, at Delos and at Athens, and a minor disturbance (involving 150 slaves) even erupted at Rome. But these and other sporadic uprisings were quickly put down. Four thousand slaves were defeated at Sinuessa, 450 crucified at Minturnae. Prompt but savage action by the authorities tended to deter others.

In Sicily, however, the revolt – for a time – continued: according to the historian Livy, Eunus' forces rose to as many as 70,000. Gradually, though, the tide turned, and the Roman general Publius Rupilius (consul in 132 BC) gained the upper hand against the rebels, and eventually crushed them. We are told that Eunus and his slaves were so hard-pressed under siege that they ate first the children, then the women, and then one another. When Eunus himself was captured, his companions in hiding, so Diodorus informs us, were a cook, a baker, his masseur and his drinking companion. Eunus himself apparently died as a result of being eaten by lice.

SPARTACUS

Spartacus' revolt is better known. A gladiator from the training school at Capua in southern Italy, Spartacus was born in Thrace and had served in an auxiliary unit of the Roman army. In 73 BC he and a few other gladiators broke out from their training school and made their base on Mount Vesuvius:

> Joined there by many runaway slaves, and even by some freedmen from country farms, he plundered the surrounding area. He was supported by his lieutenants Oenomaeus and Crixus. Since he divided the loot equally, he soon had a big following. Varinius Glaber was first sent against him, then Publius Valerius – not at the head of regular armies but with forces that had been mustered in random haste, for the Romans did not at first think of this as a war but rather as an act of brigandage or large-scale robbery. These forces attacked Spartacus but were quickly defeated, Valerius' horse being captured by Spartacus himself – so near was the Roman general to being taken prisoner by a gladiator.
>
> [Appian, *Civil Wars* I 14.116]

Spartacus now led some 70,000 slaves, and the Romans saw that they did in fact have a war on their hands. The consuls of 72 BC were despatched against him, but they too were defeated. It is said that Spartacus wanted to lead his men north and out of Italy but that they refused, preferring to stay where they were and plunder. Spartacus' force had grown to about 120,000 when in 71 BC Marcus Crassus was given the command against him. With the help of Lucullus and nearly ten legions Crassus defeated the rebellious gladiator. The writer Appian (second century AD) supplies the final details:

The remainder of Spartacus' army suffered such heavy losses that the number of dead on his side could not be counted; the Romans lost about 1,000 men. Spartacus' body was never found. Crassus pursued the main part of Spartacus' forces which were still at large in the mountains after fleeing from the battlefield and had split up into four groups, continuing to fight until all but 6,000 of them had perished. These were taken prisoner by Crassus and crucified along the whole length of the *Via Appia*, leading from Capua to Rome. [Appian, *Civil Wars* I 14.120]

It is estimated that the number of slaves involved in this war must have totalled about 150,000. The vast majority of these, as we have said, would have come from the estates, since Spartacus does not seem to have attracted the city slaves. They were rebelling against the terrible conditions on those estates and there was no question of any campaign to abolish slavery as such. Though a few slaves may have been ready to escape from Italy with Spartacus, most of them were attracted by the excitement and the lure of plunder.

12 *A still from the film* Spartacus

THE CRUCIFIXION OF SLAVES

The crucifixion of Spartacus' 6,000 was not an exceptional punishment. Slaves who revolted and were caught were regularly crucified. More significant is the large number executed on this occasion: it shows that slaves must have been comparatively easy to replace in the Republican era (as opposed to the time of the Empire), as is suggested earlier in this book. Nor is this the only example of a crucifixion on this scale during the first century BC. In 36 BC, when Octavian (the future Emperor Augustus) defeated Sextus Pompeius' fleet, he took 30,000 prisoners many of them no doubt slaves. Of these Octavian crucified 6,000, handing the rest back to their owners for punishment.

RUNAWAY SLAVES

So far this chapter has been concerned with large groups of slaves. There were, of course, numerous examples of individual slaves running away, from harsh masters, or simply because they wanted to escape from slavery. Androcles was one of these:

My master was the proconsular governor of Africa. Whilst I was there with him, I was driven to run away by the number of daily beatings I received – which I in no way deserved. To escape detection I took refuge in remote plains and deserts, intending, if I ran out of food, to kill myself in some way. But I was discovered by soldiers and taken prisoner, and then sent from Africa to my master who was now back in Rome. Without hesitation he had me condemned to death: I was to be thrown to the wild beasts in the arena.
[Aulus Gellius, V 14.17]

Even somebody like Cicero who, we have seen, was a kind master, could lose slaves, as happened when his reader Dionysius ran away. A search would be mounted for such slaves. A passage from Petronius illustrates this well:

A town-crier, accompanied by a policeman and a fair-sized crowd, entered the building and read out the following proclamation: 'Lost recently at the baths one boy, about sixteen years of age with curly hair and soft skin; a handsome lad, answering to the name of Giton. Anyone returning him or giving information that leads to his recapture will receive a reward of 1,000 sesterces.' [Petronius, *Satyricon* 97]

A public notice, dated 156 BC, from Alexandria in Egypt also mentions a reward but gives rather more detail about the slave concerned:

His name is Hermon, alias Nilus, and he is a Syrian. He is about 18 years old, of medium build, clean-shaven, and with good legs. He has a dimple on his chin, a mole on the left side of the nose, and a scar just above the left corner of his mouth. He has two letters tattooed on his right wrist ...
[*Select Papyri* (Loeb) 2. p. 137]

A profitable and sometimes crooked living was made by professional slave-hunters. In this connection, it is important to remember that sheltering a runaway slave was an offence. Later on it was also made a crime to buy or sell such a slave – rather like the law today about stolen property. The slave was, after all, his master's property, and in law an object rather than a person (see chapter 5 for the definition of a slave's legal status).

13   A slave-collar tag: Tene me ne fugia(m) et revoca me ad domnu(m) meu(m) Viventium in ar(e) a Callisti = *Stop me from running away and bring me back to my master Viventius in the yard of Callistus.*

Apart from suffering Androcles' fate, a runaway slave might have the letters F H E and the initials of his owner branded on his forehead. For example:

FHELT (standing for *Fugitivus hic est L. Titii*)
'This man is the runaway slave of Lucius Titius'.

Slave collars were another way of identifying runaway slaves. A slave who had tried to run away would have an iron or bronze collar fixed around his neck, sometimes with an identifying disc or plate attached – as on a dog collar – and inscribed with some such words as:

Restrain me so that I don't escape, and take me back to my master Pascasius in the colonnade in Trajan's market. [Dessau, *ILS* 8729]

Or, more persuasively:

I have run away, so keep hold of me. When you have returned me to my master Zoninus, you will receive a reward. [Dessau, *ILS* 8731]

A really desperate slave might commit even suicide. The following two passages from Seneca describe several ways by which slaves had succeeded in doing this, and make the practice seem a common one:

One slave threw himself off the roof to escape his master's further anger; another drove a sword into his belly to avoid recapture after running away.

Recently when a German gladiator was being prepared for the morning performance [in the arena], he jammed a sponge down his throat and, keeping his jaws clenched, suffocated himself. [Seneca, *Letters* IV 4 & LXX 20]

However, it is, on the face of it, unlikely that many slaves would have resorted to suicide as a release from their slavery and the topic is not often mentioned in the ancient writers, except by Seneca.

7

Freedom and freedmen

Many people think that all Roman slaves were treated very cruelly by their masters who beat, tortured and killed them for no apparent reason. We have seen that many slaves, particularly those working in the mines or on the great farm estates, often did suffer very harsh treatment. On the other hand, instances of cruel treatment and of slaves attacking their masters because of it were quite uncommon in the towns and cities of the Roman world. One clear bit of evidence for this friendly attitude on the part of masters towards their slaves is that slaves were frequently given their freedom by their masters through the process of manumission. 'Manumission' comes from a Latin word and means 'setting free from control'.

There were many reasons why slaves were given their freedom. Although the Romans tended to justify their position by telling themselves that other races were inferior and born to slavery, many found it hard to believe that this was really so. The Stoic philosophers taught that all men were brothers and this idea became fashionable and led many masters to treat their slaves as human beings – servants, not chattels – but not to think that they should be free. On the other hand, some masters who had once been slaves treated their own slaves very harshly.

In practice it was not the great ideas of equality and liberty which led most masters to free their slaves so much as the recognition that individual slaves deserved it. Many talented slaves who had performed outstanding services for their master were, like Tiro, rewarded with their freedom. The masters themselves often benefited by freeing slaves whose gratitude could be turned to good use. A young master may well have freed the slave-girl whom he wished to marry. The following writer suggests even worse motives:

Slaves who have assisted their masters in murders or crimes against the gods or the state are rewarded with their freedom (to prevent their being called upon to give evidence under torture). Some are freed so that they can receive the corn dole every month at state expense and give it to their former masters. Others have been freed because their masters thought it was amusing or because they wanted to be popular. I know for a fact that some men have even freed their slaves in their wills so that their funerals might be accompanied by crowds of mourners wearing caps of liberty and calling their former masters good men. [Dionysius of Halicarnassus, IV 24]

Similarly a slave who was freed while his master was still alive became a dependant or 'client' of his former master and the more clients a person had, the greater was his prestige.

The freeing of slaves on such a large scale was a source of great concern to the Emperor Augustus:

Augustus thought it was very important not to let true Roman blood be contaminated by foreign blood and so he was keen not to create new Roman citizens or to allow more than a limited number of slaves to be freed.

Not only did he make it extremely difficult for slaves to be freed and still more difficult for them to obtain full independence, by strictly regulating the number, condition and status of freed slaves; but he ruled that no slave who had ever been kept imprisoned in chains or had been tortured could become a citizen even if he had been set free by the most honourable legal ceremony.

[Suetonius, *Augustus* 40]

He was also anxious to stop the practice of masters freeing their slaves in order to put the responsibility for feeding them on to the state:

After announcing a distribution of corn, Augustus found that the number of citizens had been increased by a considerable quantity of recently freed slaves. He announced that those to whom he had promised nothing were entitled to nothing and he refused to increase the amount of the dole.

[Suetonius, *Augustus* 42]

Some poorer masters found it expensive to keep too many slaves, especially if they were old or worn out and past working. The able slaves took up the responsibility for finding their own livelihood, though they were still entitled to help from their former master, and they had to perform services for him (see p. 70). The more helpless ones, if they had been formally set free, were Roman citizens and could receive the state corn dole.

As an alternative to the gift of freedom seen in the previous examples a slave was often allowed to purchase his freedom.

Although slaves were not paid officially for the work they did for their masters, they were usually allowed to acquire small sums of money for performing various tasks. This was called their *peculium* or savings (see p. 40).

> In exchange for their freedom they pay out their savings which they have scraped together by cheating their own stomachs.
>
> [Seneca, *Letters* LXXX 4]

Slaves who were given more responsibilities by their masters were able to increase their *peculium* with profits from any business deals they were allowed to conduct. Those who were doorkeepers often took bribes to let clients in:

> We clients are forced to hand over bribes and swell the pocket-money of some trendy slave. [Juvenal, *Satires* III 88–9]

The more dishonest slaves sometimes stole to increase their *peculium*. Normally a slave bought his freedom by giving his master his own value in money but some mean-minded masters demanded more than the full market-value. Some slaves managed to acquire very large sums for their *peculium* and did not use all of it to buy freedom:

> Faustus, slave of Versennius, made arrangements for the building of a temple to Priapus from his own *peculium*. [Dessau, *ILS* 3581]

Technically the *peculium* belonged to the master since a slave could not own property, but a master respected this agreement with his slaves for common sense told that a slave who had hopes of freedom was less troublesome and worked harder. The buying of freedom using *peculium* was always a business deal and there may not often have been much good-will involved in it. It was sometimes the only way a slave was able to gain his freedom.

In all these cases the slave had to be freed or manumitted. There were two methods: 'informal manumission' and 'formal manumission'.

INFORMAL MANUMISSION

Informal manumission was not technically legal under the Republic but it avoided the 5 % tax which the government placed on all formal manumissions. By this method the slave did not gain full freedom – his master could change his mind – nor did he receive citizenship. This unsatisfactory arrangement was changed under Augustus. Informally-freed slaves became freedmen and received Latin status i.e. partial Roman citizenship. After this, informal manumission became a more popular practice.

There were three ways in which a master could set his slaves free informally. He could send the slave a letter in which he granted the slave his freedom; he could simply invite the slave to join himself and his guests at the dinner table, from which moment the slave would be free; or he could invite a few friends to his house and in their presence declare that the slave was free:

Marcus Aurelius Ammonio, son of Lupercus and Terheuta, of the ancient and famous city of Hermopolis Major, set free in the presence of friends his house-born female slave Helene, who was about thirty four years old, and ordered her to be free. He received for her freedom from Aurelius Ales, of the village of Tisichis, 2,200 imperial drachmas, which Ales made a present of to the freedwoman Helene.

Done at Hermopolis Major, July 25 in the consulship of Gratus and Seleucus [AD 221]

[SIGNATURES] I, Marcus Aurelius Ammonio, freed Helene and received 2,200 drachmas from Aurelius Ales as stated above.

I, Aurelius Ales, paid in full the 2,200 drachmas and will make no claim on the freedwoman Helene. (I Aurelius Ammonio, wrote for him because he is illiterate.) [FIRA Vol. 3, No. 11]

FORMAL MANUMISSION

Formal manumission was more complicated. A slave who had been formally manumitted became a freedman (*libertus*) but his rights as a citizen were limited. He could vote, marry and carry on trade but he could not serve in the legions, become a senator, or, with few exceptions, a knight. Nor could he hold a magistracy even in the towns of Italy. The sons of freedmen on the other hand were not subject to these restrictions.

Again there were three methods: by the rod, by the census, by the will. The first of these was a legal ceremony which took place in the presence of a praetor (or sometimes other magistrates). The master brought the slave along to the praetor who had arranged for one of his assistants to act as a 'declarer of freedom' (*assertor libertatis*). This

14   A manumission ceremony; the slave is about to be touched by the vindicta

man touched the slave with a rod (*vindicta*) and declared that he was free and was no longer the property of his master. The master did not dispute this and the praetor decided in favour of the *assertor*. The master then turned the slave round and slapped him, and from that moment the slave was a free man. It is not clear what the slap (*alapa*) was supposed to mean. Perhaps it showed the slave that he should not get too big-headed in his new position as a free man – the goddess Nemesis was always there to take him down a peg. Or perhaps it was meant to be the last insult that the slave suffered before becoming free: in either case it was a strange ceremony.

The second method, by the census, was used only during the Republic, when there were censors. Every five years the censors took on the job of drawing up lists of those who were citizens. Any master who wanted to free a slave simply ordered his name to be included on the roll of citizens. Since there were no censors under the Empire, this method died out.

The third method, by the will, was the most popular. It allowed a master to show how grateful he was for the service his slaves had given him during his lifetime. But he had to get the wording of the will right:

... As for my slave Cronio, after my death, if he has carried out all his duties properly and has handed over everything to my heir mentioned above or to my trustee, then I want him to be free and I ask that the 5 % tax be paid for him from my estate. [FIRA Vol. 3 No. 47]

By putting it in these words, the master has left it to his heir to free Cronio. So Cronio, for the time being remains legally a slave. To make sure that a slave was actually freed by the will, the master had to say something like this:

Gaius Longinus Castor, veteran honourably discharged from the Praetorian fleet of Misenum, made this will. I direct that my slave Marcella over thirty years of age, and my slave Cleopatra over thirty years of age shall be freed and they shall each in equal portion be my heirs ... My slave Sarapias, daughter of my freedwoman Cleopatra, shall be freed.

[FIRA Vol. 3 No. 50]

In this case the instructions are clear. Castor mentions the age of Marcella and Cleopatra because slaves under thirty could not be full citizens. Notice that the manumission is immediate: when Castor declares Sarapias free, he calls her mother, Cleopatra, his freed-woman, not his slave as before.

In 2 BC a law was passed (Lex Fufia Caninia) which restricted the number of slaves that could be freed under a will. This restriction was expressed as a proportion of the number of slaves a master owned: if he owned between one and ten, he could free half; between ten and thirty, one third; between thirty and one hundred, a quarter; and between one hundred and five hundred, a fifth. One hundred was the maximum a master could free under his will. In AD 4 a second law was passed (Lex Aelia Sentia) placing further restrictions on the freeing of slaves. Only masters over twenty years of age were allowed to free slaves – unless a master under twenty could show very good reasons why a slave should be freed.

Patrons and clients

The freedman still had ties with his former master who now became his patron (*patronus*). This he would acknowledge by changing the form of his name. As a slave he would have had just one name which signified either his race, a special quality or merely a favourite name given him by his master. As a freedman he usually took the first two names of his former master and added his own to it as a *cognomen*: e.g. Tiberius Claudius Diomedes.

He had various duties to perform as his former master's client (*cliens*) and these included working a number of days each year for him or offering payment instead, paying respects to his patron each morning at a special greeting ceremony (*salutatio*), accompanying him about his business and supporting him in any law cases or political elections in which he was involved. A freedman had to support his patron if he fell on hard times, and if the freedman died childless, the patron had a right to all or part of his property.

Although once free a freedman had the opportunity to choose his future career, there were many restrictions placed on his choice. If he had been lucky, he may have acquired or developed various skills while he was a slave, and these could be put to good use now that he was free. He may have had certain responsibilities under his former master which were a good training if he wanted to set himself up in a small business. Often his patron would provide the money or the premises for such a business and would receive a percentage of the profits in return. It may have been more convenient for him to remain in his former master's household as a manager, or even partner.

In any case it was often the easiest course to remain in close contact with a former master. For those who did not, the choice was almost non-existent. What skills could an odd-job man offer for employment? None of any value, except to his former master, and if his master was not very well-off himself, the freedman could expect little or no financial help. Either he was forced to remain with his master as little better than a slave or join the ranks of the unemployed citizens waiting for the corn dole.

We do know, mostly from tomb inscriptions, that those freedmen and freedwomen who were lucky enough to receive support from their masters undertook a bewildering number of careers and occupations. Firstly there were opportunities to run small businesses such as butcher, perfumer, clothier, fuller, builder, general merchant, baker, metalworker or jeweller:

To the spirits of the departed. Marcus Canuleius Zosimus; 28 years old; his patron erected this to a well-deserving freedman. During his life he spoke unkindly of no one; he did nothing without his patron's permission; there was always a great amount of gold and silver in his possession and he never desired any of it; in his craft – silver engraving in the Clodian style – he excelled everybody. [*CIL* vi 9 222]

And in the case of one baker we have a splendid monument in the form of a baker's oven. Along the top is carved a frieze showing the activities of his bakery, and along the bottom an inscription which reads:

[This is the tomb of] Marcus Vergilius Eurysaces, contract baker, as it appears. [*CIL* i 1, 203]

By which he must have meant that it was obvious to anyone looking at the monument that he was a baker.

15   A relief from the tomb of Eurysaces, a contract baker

It was also possible to find a job as a cart-driver, linen-weaver, agent or tax-farmer. Taxes in Rome were collected by individuals or companies who applied for a contract. Large-scale tax-collecting was beyond most freedmen because the sum to be collected had to be paid to the government in advance, but some of them managed to handle local taxation. We also find freedmen working as market-gardeners and horticulturalists.

Freedmen who had learned special skills as slaves or who possessed special talents were able to continue their professions when they had gained their freedom. These included auctioneers, scholars, writers, teachers, architects, painters, sculptors, surveyors and doctors:

To the spirits of the departed. To Marcus Ulpius Eutyches, imperial freedman, surveyor, his freedmen to their patron most well deserving.

[*CIL* xii 4,490]

Publius Decimius Eros Merula, freedman of Publius, clinical doctor, surgeon, oculist . . . [*CIL* xi 5,400]

16   *An oculist at work*

Many of Rome's entertainments were provided by freedmen. These included actors and stage performers, musicians and gladiators. By contrast, many freedmen and freedwomen preferred to remain in domestic service as maids, litterbearers, footmen, cooks, general odd-job men, *paedagogi* and nurses. Others put their special clerical skills to good use as letter-carriers, political attendants, clerical officers, book-copiers, secretaries, accountants, tax officials and political agents. We also find freedmen as bailiffs and managers on large farming estates; some even managed, no doubt through the support of their former masters, to become owners of farm estates.

Imperial freedmen

During the Republic the Romans elected their public officials annually; men were not normally allowed to hold office for two consecutive years. This meant in practice that they did not have much time to get to grips with the problems nor to get to know their departments and their colleagues. The situation needed a permanent staff of full-time assistants to keep the various departments running and to act as advisory centres for the annual officials. The Romans found the answer to this in their freedmen.

Freedmen were often employed by their masters as secretaries and agents in private life; it seemed obvious to use them as assistants in public service as well. They were well qualified for the job: many were well-educated and responsible people who had acted as financial agents for their patrons in private life. Many were Greek-speaking and were, therefore, useful to officials who had provinces to govern in the East; indeed they were often more talented than ordinary free-born Roman citizens.

A CIVIL SERVICE

By the time of the Emperor Claudius (AD 41–54) the services of these freedmen assistants had developed into a full-scale civil service. As a permanent body they had a great advantage over the officials elected every year. Even under the Republic we learn from Cicero that the freedmen were in a very powerful position:

The laws are those which our staff want. [Cicero, *The Laws* III 46]

I notice several magistrates who, ignorant of the law, know only as much as their staff want them to know. [Cicero, *The Laws* III 48]

It was quite often the case that the permanent staff were never interfered with by the officials they were serving. We can see how easy it was for certain individual freedmen to become very powerful behind the scenes while still being officially the servants of the free-born magistrates. Cicero saw the dangers of letting slaves and ex-slaves become involved in public life. This is his advice to his brother:

And if one of your slaves proves outstandingly loyal, let him be involved in private and domestic matters; but do not let him become concerned with affairs connected with your public duty or with public business.

[Cicero, *Letters to his brother Quintus* I 1.17]

17   The tombstone of Titus Flavius Stephanus, an imperial freedman in charge of the camels

LICINUS

Augustus, the first emperor, allowed freedmen to take on positions of great responsibility as well as to serve in the fleets and in the fire brigades. He entrusted the financial administration of Aquitania and Lugdunensis in Gaul to the freedmen Licinus very early on in his reign:

Augustus behaved strictly but kindly towards his dependants and slaves, and honoured some of his freedmen, such as Licinus, Celadus and others, with his close intimacy. [Suetonius, *Augustus* 67]

Licinus is reported to us as being arrogant, cheating the natives and generally misusing his position of trust:

His trickery went so far that in some cases where the people paid their tribute monthly, he made the months fourteen in number, saying that December was really the tenth month and so they must count two more (which he called the eleventh and twelfth) as the last and pay the money that was due for these months. [Dio, *Roman History* 54.21]

In fact Licinus' wealth was proverbial:

What point is there in being a Senator when members of old Roman families have to take up sheepfarming for a living, while I, a freedman, own more money than even Pallas or Licinus. [Juvenal, *Satires* I 109]

Even after his death, his tomb was extravagant enough to be mentioned in another satirical poem:

Licinus lies in a marble tomb; yet Cato has none and Pompey only a tiny one; and we still believe the gods exist? [Anthology, 77]

Perhaps the bad reports were exaggerated. Licinus is very probably an example of a freedman who enjoyed a successful career, which may not have been completely honest, but who suffered from the contempt that free-born Romans tended to hold for men of inferior status in positions of power and importance.

THE FATHER OF CLAUDIUS ETRUSCUS

A freedman whose career was blameless and highly successful is known to us only from a poem written to his son, Claudius Etruscus, to console him for the death of his father. We do not even know his name, but his career is important, because it shows us clearly to what heights freedmen could rise.

He was born in A D 2 or 3 in Smyrna in Asia Minor. He came to Italy as a slave during the reign of Tiberius:

You entered the palace of Tiberius while your young face had hardly shown the first signs of early manhood.

He was manumitted at the age of thirty during the last years of Tiberius. The next emperor, Gaius, continued to employ his services:

... nor did the next emperor, although cruel and insane, banish you. You accompanied him, although you were in ill-health, to the frozen North [on Gaius' expedition to Britain] ...
... But Claudius [the next emperor] raised you for your services to the highest office in his old age.

This last statement probably means that Claudius gave him a position of great responsibility within the imperial civil service. We are not sure what he was doing during Nero's reign (A D 54–68) but it seems that he was away from Rome in the East, probably on some financial mission. He returned to Rome in A D 70 and was appointed controller of the Imperial Treasury (*libertus a rationibus*) by the Emperor Vespasian:

Now he alone was in control of the sacred treasure, wealth drawn from every country, the revenue of the Empire. All the wealth from the Spanish gold mines, from the African wheatfields, from the pearl fisheries of the eastern seas, from the ivory trade of India ... He is quick to reckon the requirements of the Roman army, the amount of the free corn supply, the money required for the repair of roads, temples, aqueducts and harbours; he is also in charge of the finances for the decorations of imperial palaces, statues and of the production of money at the Imperial Mint. [Statius, *Silvae* III 3]

Three years later he was given the honour by Vespasian of being allowed to become a member of the equestrian class. He was exiled by the next emperor, Domitian in A D 82/3 but we are not told the reason. He was allowed to return in A D 90 and he died two years later at the age of 90.

NARCISSUS

Narcissus was one of the most influential freedmen during the reign of the Emperor Claudius (A D 41–54). He occupied the post of *libertus*

76

ab epistulis, which means he was head of the department which dealt with all the imperial correspondence. Together with his colleagues, Pallas and Callistus, he held the most powerful position in the Empire next to the emperor himself.

Narcissus first exercised his power in the removal of the emperor's third wife, Messalina, and later took part in the execution. After Messalina had been executed, Claudius married Agrippina, his niece. Because Narcissus had supported the claims of a rival woman, he was hated by Agrippina, and after she had killed Claudius and put her son, Nero, in his place, she lost no time in killing Narcissus as well. Further details of Narcissus' story may be read in Tacitus *Annals XI–XIII*.

The careers of Licinus, the father of Claudius Etruscus and Narcissus show us clearly how it was possible for men of such different characters to profit greatly in the imperial service and, sometimes, to meet their downfall.

HONOURS FOR FREEDMEN

Whether freedmen worked for the government or privately, they had many opportunities for establishing themselves as full and useful citizens. In particular they were allowed to occupy two religious positions: *vicomagistri*, who were entrusted with keeping order in the city and superintending the worship of Stata Mater, a goddess who protected Rome against fire; and *seviri Augustales*, who were appointed to organise the worship of the emperor and hold games in his honour. With all political offices barred to them, freedmen regarded these two positions as the highest level of public service to which they could aspire. In this way freedmen were able to serve the community and earn the respect of their fellow-citizens, something not possible for them to do as slaves.

8
Conclusion

Abolition?

No-one in the ancient world would have dreamt of actually abolishing slavery since, as we have seen, slavery was an integral and accepted part of life at that time. The great slave revolts were not part of a move to abolish slavery but merely to improve conditions for slaves. The majority of Romans (as the Greeks before them) saw no injustice in some races being treated as inferior to others. Even though many educated, thinking Romans realised that slaves were human beings who must have some basic rights, even if they were merely property in Roman law, no-one supported a campaign for the abolition of slavery. It may be that the whole situation was not as intolerable as we are often led to believe – manumission was, despite legislation, very commonplace, and since (as we mentioned in chapter 1), by the time of Domitian, some ninety per cent of Rome's population could trace some freedmen in their ancestry, it may be that freedom did not have the same attraction and meaning as it has for us.

It would be convenient to say that when Christianity was established as the Roman state religion, slavery died away because all Christians believed in the brotherhood of man which made it impossible for one to be the slave of another. Unfortunately, this is very far from the truth. It seems that the early Christians saw no difficulty in accepting slavery as a fact of life and, while many of the earliest Christians had been slaves who were looking for a religion which promised hope for even the lowest of men and women, there were no moves to abolish the idea of slavery when Christianity was accepted. In fact the Christian emperor Justinian, who completely reorganised and codified Roman law, had assembled in the sixth century such a complete collection of laws governing slavery that they were used as much of the justification for the slave trade over a thousand years later.

Improvements in technology

Some people believe that slavery prevented the Romans from improving their industries and technology. They argue there was no need for the Romans to invent machinery because there were always enough slaves to do the work by hand.

Two direct examples of machines being used to perform work more efficiently and quickly should be enough to correct this idea. The first is the North Gallic reaping machine, described by Pliny the Elder. It must have been a great advantage to farmers. The second is the crane which must have speeded up building methods considerably. What we do see are slaves being used to gain the best advantage from machines of this kind.

The end of Roman slavery

Slavery, then, was never abolished. It died out for various reasons, some more obvious than others. Firstly, as more and more countries were conquered by the Romans and became part of the Empire, the sources of slaves became fewer. This meant that the slave population relied on home-breeding to continue providing slaves for the market. Inevitably many masters found it increasingly difficult to keep up their numbers of slaves and were forced to find other ways of getting the work done on their estates. During the later part of the Roman Empire there was a definite change in the social structure and we see two distinct classes of Roman citizens emerging – upper and lower. The laws of the time seem to treat the lower class quite differently from the upper class, even to the point of regarding them as little better than slaves and deserving of slave punishments. The lower class were often forced by their poverty and lack of rights to find security in working on the large estates. Owners quickly found that here was a ready source of labour, not slaves, but free men who had to work to survive. Especially for this last reason slavery gradually died out and tenant-farming, which was to be the foundation of the feudal systems of the Middle Ages, became more common.

Index